How To Become A Mail Order Millionaire

How To Become A Mail Order Millionaire

BY FRED BROITMAN

Superior Press
333 N Michigan Avenue • Suite 1032
Chicago, IL 60601
Phone 312.726.3141 • Fax 312.726.3142

Published by: Superior Press, Chicago, Illinois

ISBN-13 978-0-9779619-1-7
ISBN-10 0-9779619-1-5

Printed in the United States of America

Cover Photo: © Trinette Reed/Blend

Dedication

To my wife, Charlotte and our three sons, David, Ben, and Jeff, who have always provided me with love and inspiration. Without my family's cooperation and understanding, this book would remain unwritten.

Fred Broitman
Chicago, IL 2010

Contents

Introduction

This book could very easily have been subtitled "Everything You Ever Wanted To Know About Mail Order...But Didn't Even Know What To Ask!"

The book is designed to guide the beginner on the road to success in his or her very own mail order business. In simple terms. To provide a "road map" so easy to follow that even the most unsophisticated newcomer to the field can chart a path from Point A (deciding to go ahead) to Point B (pot-of-gold success)! To give you a wealth of time-tested pointers you won't find anywhere else. To provide you with loads of stimulating and thought-provoking ideas.

Or, if you are already involved in a business, to show you how to turn your existing experience and expertise into big bucks, by expanding into mail order.

In my many years of mail order counseling, I have constantly run across oft-told myths and misunderstandings about mail order. What I will also try to do in this book is eliminate those myths and set out in a clear and concise manner, how to go about starting your own mail order business and how to do it for very small dollars. How you can get started right in your own home. In short, how you can become a success – literally become a self-made millionaire – in your own mail order business!

The formula for success to be found in this book has been culled by the major principal of one of the nation's leading mail order advertising agencies, Fred Broitman of Sunman Direct, a Chicago advertising agency in business for over 30 years. Mr. Broitman has been personally responsible for supervising and creating advertising that has produced millions upon millions of dollars in sales for many of the most successful mail order advertisers in the country. Many of these companies started out with a single test ad in a single magazine.

Fred Broitman is approached daily for advice by many people who want to get into the mail order business. Corporate executives, entrepreneurs, ordinary men and women who have a product or offer a service which they believe has mail order potential, folks who have invented a promising item or just an idea for one, and people who have found or created a unique product which they have sold successfully in their own community and now wish to sell by mail all over the world.

These men and women frequently ask questions like: How do I get started? What makes a good mail order product or offer? How much should I price my product for? If I spend $10,000 on an ad, and I run in a publication that has 1,000,000 circulation, am I going to get a 10% response and make $2,000,000? How soon after I run the ad am I going to know whether it is a success?

The answers to all these questions and countless others are to be found in the pages that follow. Mail order can truly be a golden pathway to success. Like any road, there are curves, roadblocks, and sidetracks that can confuse and misdirect the traveler who attempts to do it all on his own. This book attempts to provide an easy to follow road map leading to the land of the Mail Order Millionaires. Good luck on the journey.

Fred Broitman
Chicago, Illinois
July 2010

Chapter

1

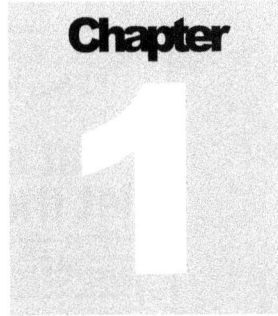

How to Start Your Own Mail Order Business From Scratch

"The creation of a thousand forests is in one acorn." – Ralph Waldo Emerson

The ad on the following page promotes one specific direct marketing opportunity. It is shown here because it conveys a "generic" message – what it promises could apply to most mail order business opportunities.

1- Pase Sample Advertisement

Mail order has been called at times "The Store Without a Door", "The Store Without Walls" or "The Store That Never Closes".

The real beauty of the mail order business is that everybody wins. The consumer wins. The mail order marketer wins.

First, take a look at the consumer. Mail order shopping, whether through advertising, catalogs, mailings, TV or the Internet, is a great way to browse, the most convenient way to shop.

Shopping by mail can save the buyer money, with excellent values. Shopping by mail also saves the cost of gasoline, and the frustration of finding parking close by, as well as the bother and wasted time of standing in lines at stores, dealing with surly and disinterested clerks (if you can find them). Mail order shopping eliminates hassles, such as fighting the crowds, jostling elbows with other shoppers, and juggling packages under your arms.

Best of all, the mail order shopper can do his or her shopping at home, sitting in their easy chair in their living room, at their own leisure and convenience.

Relaxing at home the mail order shopper can find exotic jewelry or perfumes from around the world, clothing from Scotland or the Orient, art treasures, gourmet food, games for their children, sporting and camping wear, books and magazines, special videos, automotive supplies, a business of your own…you name it! Virtually anything or everything you want or need for yourself or your family, for your home, for your friends and associates, for your life.

The mail order shopper can go on a shopping spree without ever leaving his or her living room. 24 hours a day, 7 days a week.

The mail order marketer wins because he or she can start a business with a minimum of effort and money. They can work out of the home, starting out modestly. Even develop the business spare time, continuing with a regular job until the mail order business has been established and developed enough to become a full-time career. Or the mail business can be used as an extra money maker that another family member can operate once it's up and running.

I urge you to take a moment now to go back and read the Pase ad shown at the beginning of the chapter. You'll learn a lot from reading every word in this ad.

This ad has been fabulously successful! Can you guess why? Quite simply because it offers the reader what everybody who considers getting into a new business of their own wants. First look at what is called the "eyebrow" message (it's called that because it sits above the main headline). The eyebrow promises the reader regular earnings of an extra $800 to $2,500 a week with little effort. Wouldn't you like to earn extra money like this? Who wouldn't?

Now look at the headline itself: "JUST SIT BACK, RELAX AND LET THE MONEY ROLL IN!" Wow, what a dramatic promise of what every mail order beginner dreams of. The message is irresistible!

Further down in the copy you read: "Most of today's big money-making opportunities involve a lot of time and hard work...you have to work hard instead of work smart to get anywhere! But with this amazing opportunity, the money comes in even when you're asleep, away on vacation or on your own boat reeling in the big one at your favorite fishing spot!"

This ad tells the whole story of why anyone would want to get into mail order, in a nutshell!

Yes, mail order marketing is an easy way to be your own boss. To own an exciting money-making business of your own. It can enable you to bring all your dreams to reality. Provide you with the means to travel to exciting places like Hawaii, Paris, Rome...own your own boat, a snappy sports car or motor home...lavish jewelry and furs on yourself or those you love...spend more time hunting and fishing or playing golf…provide extra money for educating your children. Yes, your own mail order business can make all your dreams of financial independence, security, and the good life come true.

Lest we lead you down the garden path…as any economist will tell you, there is no such thing as a "free lunch". Don't consider going into your own mail order business unless you are willing to work twice as hard for half the pay to get yourself established. But at the same time, remember your psychic pay can give you more satisfaction than any paycheck. And the reward down the road can be tremendous.

First of all, you want to pick an item to promote through mail order which has a good chance for success (we will tell you what to look for in a later chapter). But one thing you want to keep in mind is that many financial experts advise that your odds of success may well have less to do with the product you offer than they do with your drive, enthusiasm and realistic business approach. Don't expect success to happen automatically, and don't count on anyone else. Successful mail order marketers are self-made entrepreneurs. They did everything themselves at the outset. They invested long hours, long days and long weeks at the beginning, to build up their businesses successfully. It's an education. Trial and error. They learned through experience, they gleaned through "the textbook of life" what can't be derived from any published books.

If you'll ask yourself a few simple questions, you'll increase your chance for success in mail order:

1. What is the market for your product or service?

2. Does your product meet that market need?

3. What kind of competition will you have?

4. Is your product better than any of the others? Or is it different?

5. What will the product cost you to purchase, or to produce?

6. How much will it cost you to advertise or promote by mail order?

7. Do you have money or access to enough money to keep the business going until it becomes self-sufficient?

8. How many orders will you need to make a go of it?

How To Go About Getting Start-Up Money

Chances are you won't need outside help to get started. Two out of three new businesses don't. You may already have money in the bank, at least enough to tide you over until orders start coming in. But there are other money sources available, if you need it, which some people overlook.

Your Bank. Getting a bank loan might be a lot easier than you think. Just remember that the bank needs you as much as you need them. After all, making loans is why they're in business. They want to give you a loan, if only you can give them good reason. And you've got good reason. Your chances improve when you have some sort of collateral, someone who will guarantee your loan, or can show you have good credit.

S.B.A. The Small Business Administration will often guarantee start-up loans. There is some paperwork involved, but it can be well worth the effort. State and local organizations may also provide this kind of guarantee. You can call the Small Business Administration toll-free at 1-800-368-5855 to get the background information you need. Website: http://www.sba.gov

Insurance Policies.

People often overlook the fact that their ordinary life insurance policies have a built-in loan feature. It's called the "Cash value". What this means, simply, is that when you pay your regular premiums, part of the money is set aside in case you want to borrow it back from the insurance company.

Quite literally this is your money. So you can tell the insurance company to give it back to you any time you want it, no questions asked. Technically you are taking the money back as a loan against the amount the insurance company will have to pay out to your survivors when you die. One of the nice things about borrowing against your insurance policy "Cash Value" is that you will enjoy a lower rate of interest than you would have to pay for other loans.

Another great feature is that you never have to pay the loan back, if you don't want to, or are unable to. The amount you borrow and the interest due on it will merely be deducted from the eventual payout to your survivors, if you haven't repaid the loan.

Credit Cards. If you have trouble getting a loan, consider using your credit card. Just remember that the interest rates are higher than conventional loans, but if you don't need a lot of money and you think you can pay it back quickly, this is a way many beginners choose to go.

Borrow on Your Home. You've probably built up some equity in your home. If you have, you should be able to borrow against this equity. Just be aware that if things don't work out and you can't repay the loan, you may jeopardize your home ownership.

Professional and Private Venture Capitalists. There are companies and individuals who are in business to help others get started, by furnishing start-up capital. Be aware that they will scrutinize your proposal with a magnifying glass. They will be interested only if they think you can make it really big...and they'll not only want their money back with interest, but they'll want a piece of the action. They may even want control of your business.

If you are interested in pursuing this avenue, check out Pratt's Guide to Venture Capital Sources at your library. It's published by Venture Economics in Wellesley Hills, MA..

Wealthy People in Your Own Community. And there are rich individuals who have an adventurous spirit and like to invest some of their money in start-ups like yours. Actually, they probably have twice as much cash available as the professionals. To track such individuals down you might get in touch with the Association of Venture Clubs, 265 East 100 South, Suite 300 Salt Lake City, UT 84110-3358 Tel (801)364-1100 Or the International Venture Capital Institute, P.O. Box 1333, Stamford, CT 06902 Website: http://www.vcinstitute.org . Or the Venture Capital Network, P.O. Box 882, Durham, NH 03824. Tel (603)862-3558

Mail order is a business where everybody wins. The consumer wins. The mail order marketer wins. The following chapters will help you decide if mail order marketing is for you, and if so, how to maximize your chances of becoming successful at it.

Chapter

2

How to Find
Great Mail
Order Products

"I'm gonna make him an offer he can't refuse." – Don Corleone

When you're looking for something, and you're not specific, somehow you never find it. And looking for a mail order product is no different. When you least expect it, that's when you'll run across it. Most of the time it will be staring you right in the face and you won't even realize it...those usually are the best ones.

But don't expect it to fall out of the sky either. You have to first find the right product or service and then think about ways you can develop it into a mail order offer.

A mail order "product" doesn't always mean a tangible product. Think in terms of a mail order "offer" instead of a mail order product.

Let me give you an example. Let's say you come across a watch. (Forget about the costs, marketing, etc.). You decide to sell the watch for $19.95. So your mail order product is a watch, but to make the sale of the watch more attractive and to induce more sales, you "offer" the watch with a Lifetime Guarantee and a 60 day Free Trial. Now, that's an offer.

So think in terms of mail order offers, not necessarily products.

Mail order offers can be made up of products, services, business opportunities or free information (to capture a qualified inquiry and then later convert that inquiry into a sale).

There was a mail order offer which was very successful several years ago. It operated without any inventory, had virtually no overhead and made tons of money for its owner.

The company was called "Martha's Rare Bargain News". The proprietress collected data on various hard-to-find, unusual and discounted goods. She then printed them up in a newsletter she formulated and mailed out to a list. For example: she would check out the classified ads and find an ad that offered a 100 foot vessel for $9,000.00 or a government jeep for $59.00. In the newsletter she would reprint the classified ad minus the address or phone number as to where to buy it. If you were interested in an item you would send $3.00 for two items. $5.00 for three items, or $10.00 for six items. Martha would send the address and/or phone number to you, the reader, to contact the advertiser. This provided interesting news for many people and a service for others. Especially if you lived in a small town. Certainly most local papers wouldn't carry the many different items that are sold by classified ads. Now that's creative thinking.

Finding a good mail order product might come from re-creating what is already out there.

A colleague of mine developed a mail order product a number of years ago from an existing product. We changed the formula a little and created a new name. We developed a great offer and marketed it to a completely new audience. The results were fantastically successful.

Originally, a company down south manufactured a fishing scent, that when applied to live or artificial bait, made catching fish very, very easy – even for the most inexperienced of fishermen.

Any good fisherman knows that you should use a glove or oil rag when handling your lure. Studies show that fish are repelled by human scent.

The fish were attracted when this product was sprayed on the lure because it masked the human scent. (Since most people don't use a glove or oil rag.) Secondly, it had a scent that fish were attracted to. So combined, it attracted fish to your lure and it kept them from swimming away because there was no foreign odor.

The product was originally being marketed primarily to fishermen. Naturally, they were the target market. So this company advertised in fishing and hunting books. Small ads consistently appeared in these publications offering one tube for $6 with a 30 day money back guarantee.

There it was. Staring us in the face. Here was an opportunity to take an existing product, make it better, create an offer – or at least a better offer – find a new market to go after so that it could be purchased by millions of people who might never have considered themselves fishermen, and by doing all this we hoped to develop a successful mail order product.

We went to a local chemist and had him develop a similar but better formula. We named it "Catch Fish Like Crazy" because that's what we guaranteed it would do. Our offer was in fact, just that. Buy "Catch Fish Like Crazy" and if you didn't catch fish like crazy (and that could mean anything), then simply return the unused can or cans and we'll refund your money in full. What could be fairer than that? We also created a multi-order discount if you bought more than one can. Later, we tested a free give away on orders of 4 cans or more. It worked like crazy, too!

We decided since our competition was going after the professional fisherman, we would go after the novice fisherman. We also knew that fishing was the #1 sport in America. We guessed that there were more non-professional fishermen than professional. So why not advertise in everything *but* the fishing and hunting books.

So, instead of running the ad in Hunting and Fishing News we ran it in Parade Magazine, and instead of Fur-Fish-Game we went in the American Legion. Fact is, the people who read those magazines fish too.

We wrote an ad with a headline, "Catch Fish Like Crazy" and put a story approach to it. It took a full page to tell the story and for the offer to be understood. We also knew the importance of a coupon in an ad. Our competition was trying to do it all with a small ad.

We added a lot of mystery and excitement to that ad and needed the room to do it. By the time you finished reading this ad, you had no reason not to order. You were either going to Catch Fish Like Crazy or get your money back.

The ad, the media, the offer, and the product were a huge success. Our sales were almost $1,000,000 a year.

The competition still continued to use their ads in the fishing books. Neither of us stepped on each other's toes. We never had any contact with them or they with us.

So finding a mail order product can come from something that already exists, but marketed completely differently. And like in the case of Martha's Rare Bargain News, taking and creating something brand new.

It's very rare, unless you are an inventor, to successfully create a product, manufacture it or have it manufactured, and be able to market it. The last thing you want to do is take a product that exists or has just come into the marketplace (trendy products) and decide you're going to sell it! Chances are it won't work.

Keep these guidelines in mind.

A. A product should be *exclusive*. You just can't sell Kleenex by mail, especially when you can go into any store and buy it.

B. A product/service/offer has to be *priced to offer a value and make a profit*. Catch Fish Like Crazy costs $0.68. That included the can, the mailing package, and the formula. It sold for $6.00 a can plus postage and handling. You can't always have a 9x mark-up, but to become a mail order millionaire you need a big margin.

C. Most of all, you need a product that provides a *benefit*. A cure is much better than a prevention. That's why it's difficult to sell fire extinguishers successfully in mail order. A fire extinguisher "prevents" fires from spreading, but unless you've recently had a fire, you seldom think about the need for one. On the other hand, if your feet constantly hurt, a foot pain relief remedy will immediately get your attention and probably your order too.

Often times you come across a product idea. Just like inventors do. If so, do a little research to see if such a product already exists, what does it sell for and check your list...does it fit the criteria; exclusivity, price and benefit.

If you feel it does, then give thought to your offer. How can you offer this product so that anyone who comes in contact with it can't resist ordering it?

Search out manufacturers to see how you can get this developed. If it's a product, then how can it be made? If it's a service, then who would help you develop it?

Write out all the pros and cons and set it aside for a couple of days and look at it later to see if your feelings are still as strong.

Share it with close friends or family for their reaction. But remember, this is called a mother-in-law survey. And it doesn't really mean too much!

Can you see us telling our friends about Catch Fish Like Crazy? They thought *we* were crazy. To this day, when we tell the story people laugh! You see, our friends and family were not Catch Fish Like Crazy customers.

Your idea most likely is unique to you and hopefully your customers. So take what friends and family say with a grain of salt…still, you might find some good ideas from sharing it with them. If you're convinced your idea is right, trust your instincts and go for it.

Always remember:

Exclusivity!

Pricing!

Benefit!

Chapter

3

How to Make Your Mail Order Business Profitable From the Start

"Those who trust to chance must abide by the results of chance." – Calvin Coolidge

Return on Investment (ROI)… that's the question you need to ask yourself. How much do I want back on my investment? Investment of knowledge, investment of time, investment of ideas, and investment of dollars.

Investment in dollars is the easiest one to determine. If you invested $10,000 in the bank, depending on which type of instrument you invested in…you would get, for example, a 1% return. In one year you would make $100. If you invested $100,000, your return on investment would be $1,000 for the year.

Immediately you can see that if you don't make more than 1% return on your investment in the mail order business, then you're better off putting your money in the bank.

Through several examples explained later in this chapter you will see how return on investment can be made back in less time than one year. That's what makes the mail order business exciting.

Certainly if you are profitable, the money you make will compensate you for your investment of time, knowledge and ideas.

Depending, of course, on whether your mail order business is going to be a full-time or part-time venture, your needs in financial terms will be different.

One of the beauties of this business is that you can operate it at any time, almost anywhere.

RETURN ON INVESTMENT IN SPACE ADS OR DIRECT MAIL

The formula is easy. Take the cost of all promotions, cost of goods, costs in the mail, and deduct the dollars generated from this effort to determine profit or loss. Here's a simple, but true example.

This is how it worked for Catch Fish Like Crazy. The product cost $0.68 a unit. And let's say we decide to run a Jr. Page ad in the National Enquirer, at a cost of $10,150 for one insertion. The response comes in over a period of a year, and even longer but the bulk of the response is seen within the first two months; the first 10 days' mail being the largest share.

But even before we run the ad we determine how many units we need to sell to break even.

Divide the cost of the space by the difference between your cost in the mail and what you sell the product for.

Catch Fish Like Crazy = $0.68 – sells for $6.00
Postage and Handling = $0.82
In The Mail Cost $1.50

$6.00 - $1.50 = $4.50
$10,150 / $4.50 = 2,255

2,255 is the number of units you need to sell to break even....anything beyond that is profit. Your total out-of-pocket cost would be paid for at that point.

Therefore, if the ad ran and you sold 2,500 cans, then the bottom line result would be 245 units above break-even or $1,102.50 net profit. Your return on investment would be 11.19% and you made over 11% on this one ad in less than one year. Remember, your investment in the bank made 1% profit, but it did so after one full year. On the "Catch Fish" ad we made an 11% *plus* profit and did so in just a few months.

Direct Mail is no different. Just total your costs to mail and determine how many units you need to break even.

By doing this it also helps your inventory control. You know, based on the dollars you plan on spending, how much inventory you need to keep on hand. Or how much printing you need to order.

It is meaningless to try to predict how many units you think your ad will sell or, after the ad runs, determine the percentage of response you got in relation to circulation.

Except in the case of direct mail.

In space advertising you buy ads in publications with specified circulations.

If the National Enquirer has 1,000,000 circulation, 1% response would be 10,000. This might not seem to be a difficult goal to achieve, but you probably wouldn't get a 1% return. And when you do run the ad, assuming it is profitable and you get 2,500 orders as in the Catch Fish Like Crazy example, the second time you run it, response will probably not be the same. It could be less, it could be more. There are many factors that determine how an ad will pull. Time of the year, position in the magazine, competition, etc.

In direct mail, the same holds true, except it is helpful to determine what percentage of return you need in a direct mail campaign to break even.

For example, if you are mailing 10,000 names it's easy to determine what percentage you need to get back, 2% or 3% return. A 2% return on a 10,000 mailing would result in 200 sales…at 3%, 300 sales.

These percentages can be helpful in analyzing several different lists to tell how well they did. Sometimes a mailing to the same list will result in a different percentage, but when analyzing you look at the percentage results and you can then determine as a whole how your mailing did.

But, it still boils down to the same thing; *was your ad or mailing profitable?*

And it should be pointed out, the dollars directly made from an ad or mailing aren't the only basis for determining profitability. The value of a customer or name over a period of time should be part of the return on investment.

If you've provided a customer with good service and a product, he/she is likely to reorder or buy something else from you.

At that point your advertising cost is little to nothing and your profit margin is higher.

When you build a list of customers, for yourself, you can in turn rent those names to other companies and profit from that as well.

Now you can factor these additional sales into your profit picture.

Often times during the course of a given year you should analyze these findings to determine your entire profit picture.

How many reorders did you get? How many customers repeat and buy other items from you? How many referral customers do you get? Do you sell them related goods after the initial sale, and what does that total? How much do you make off the list rental on the names you've acquired? Are you segmenting them into inquirers, buyers, hotline, etc?

The question of how much profit is proper depends on your needs, your time and effort and your determination to build a business rather then just shooting for the immediate winner.

The mail order business is just that, a business, and often time people become shortsighted and forget to look at the big picture.

A classic example which is a true story: an entrepreneur who develops health and beauty aids is constantly coming up with new products and testing them in various marketing campaigns; publications, direct mail, catalogs, continuity programs and so forth. Just after he has tested one offer he moves off that to come up with another, always looking for a big winner.

He never analyzes his business activity or approaches it with a sensible return on investment plan. He is constantly looking for the one time big winner.

When in fact, 30% or 40% of his offers could be fine tuned into long term winners.

But in his eyes the profit he is shooting for is greater than he sees with all those results, so he continues to try and re-invent the wheel.

He does run a profitable and successful business or he wouldn't be able to continue year after year. But much of his profits come from non-mail order segments of his business. Remember to look at the entire return on investment, keeping in mind building value to a name and determine your profitability based on how well you do over a period of time.

Chapter

4

What Should Your Product Sell For?

"Deals work best when each side gets something it wants from the other" –
Donald Trump

Strange as it may seem, the price of the offer is one of the last things people think about when they consider going into their own mail order business. They get all excited about their product. "I've got a sure thing. I just know it!" Next they start thinking about how to promote it. And the last thing they think about is how much should they charge for it? It seems to leave a big question mark, because they have no idea how to go about pricing their product.

Yet when it comes right down to it, price can make you or break you in mail order! Set the price too high and you won't get enough orders. Set the price too low and you rob yourself of profits. And after all, the reason you go into the mail order business is to make as much money as you possibly can.

You may have read some other books on mail order. But chances are you've never seen one that really went into the subject of pricing your offer. Even one of the classic mail order "bibles", which is over 1,500 pages long, covers every conceivable subject except how to price your offer.

When setting a price, the tendency of beginners is to think in terms of the basic cost of the product itself. "If my product costs me $4.00, I can sell it for $5.00 and make $1.00 profit – that's 25% and that's pretty good!" Remember that mail order is an advertising/promotion intensive business. By that we mean it's conceivable that it can cost you as much or more to obtain an order as it does to make or purchase the product itself.

That's why you should look for a product whose perceived value is far greater than its actual cost.

Now let's get down to the actual details. As a rule of thumb, merchandise should be marked up three or four to one, even higher if possible. In other words, if it costs you $5.00 to get the product in your hands, you should charge the buyer at least $15 or $20. And to this you can add a charge for shipping and handling. For higher priced items, say those that cost you over $25, you may mark them up only two to three times cost, since the actual dollar profit per sale is much higher.

And when you are selling through a catalog, the mark-up does not have to be as high; two times mark up is sufficient.

To help you arrive at what you should charge, keep in mind that there are certain magic Price Points. A Price Point is the point at which you begin to meet significant customer resistance. When you go above this resistance level, orders will drop off appreciably. For instance, a price of $20.50 is far less acceptable than $19.95. You see $19.95 is under $20, which is a psychological barrier point. Thus, $19.95 becomes one Price Point.

The way to determine the optimum Price Point for any product is to test it at different prices. You want to get the greatest profit return for every advertising dollar you spend. Therefore, it is conceivable that you might sell twice as many items at a $9.95 price as you would at a $14.95 price, yet depending on the arithmetic, because you make less profit per item, you might be better off at the higher price point, ending up with fewer orders, but more total profit dollars in your pocket.

On the other hand, consumers might feel a price of $14.95 for a particular item seems so far out of line that it severely limits sales, while that same product at $9.95 might attract a larger number of buyers. The only way you are going to find the best price point on any product is by testing it at various prices, keeping meticulous records of all costs, and income received, and then base your decision on all the facts.

Based on my extensive mail order experience, here are some of the most effective prices for mail order selling:

MAGIC PRICE POINT	IDEAL COST OF GOODS
$7.95 plus $1 shipping and handling	$2.25
$14.95 plus $2 shipping and handling	$3.00
$19.95 plus $3 shipping and handling	$4.50
$39.95 plus $3 shipping and handling	$10.00
$69.95 plus $3 shipping and handling	$25.00
$97.50 plus $5 shipping and handling	$35.00
$134.50 with shipping and handling FREE	$50.00
$195.00 with shipping and handling FREE	$75.00

Don't be timid about charging for shipping and handling. Almost everyone in mail order does it and your buyer expects to pay extra for this service. Keep in mind that people are more willing to pay $19.95 plus $3 shipping and handling (which comes to a total of $22.95) than they are to pay $22.95 for the product with no charge for shipping and handling. True, the end price comes out the same, but there is a big psychological difference – you have crossed over the $20 product price barrier, which will result in fewer sales. It may not be logical, but it is a fact of life and the sooner you learn to accept it, the sooner you'll be on your way to becoming a Mail Order Millionaire.

Another way to increase your results is to go for multiple orders. Your best prospect is one who has already decided he or she wants to take advantage of your offer – so capitalize on this by giving this person an incentive to increase the size of his or her order. Give them a price break on every additional item they order at the same time. You can easily afford to do this, because you have already included the total advertising/promotion cost involved in pricing of the first unit. So all additional sales after this involve only the cost of the goods alone.

Here is how to handle this. Say you are selling electrically heated socks at $19.95 a pair plus $3 shipping and handling (total $22.95). On a straight full price basis, two pair would cost $39.30 plus $6 shipping and handling (total $45.90). But, as an incentive to double the size of the order, you could advertise "BUY TWO PAIR – SAVE $8.00…only $34.90 plus $3 shipping and handling". Or not only reduce the price, but make the shipping and handling cost free: i.e.: "BUY TWO PAIR – SAVE $10.00…only $35.90, FREE shipping and handling".

THE BOTTOM LINE: HOW MUCH DID IT COST YOU? HOW MUCH MONEY DID IT BRING IN?

When all is said and done, this is what it's all about. Income versus cost. What's left over is your profit. It's that simple. And you'll never know the answer unless you keep good records. Of course, to start out with, you will be running only one ad in one or two publications, so it will be easy to keep track of all your out-of-pocket expenses (including the cost of the product itself). And you will know how many inquiries/sales your offer brought in. If you made more money than you spent, you're ahead of the game. If it cost you more than you brought in, you've had some fun and a great educational experience.

If you come close to breaking even, you may want to consider making some adjustments in your advertising or your pricing or the publications you advertised in to see if you can't turn your offer into a winner by re-testing.

But if it comes nowhere near paying off, bite the bullet, and start looking for another product.

If you think you've got a product that will be a winner, go ahead and test it. You'll never find out whether it's any good if you don't. But don't go crazy spending a lot of money to roll out with lots of ad placements. Find out if your product really has mail order potential first, by running just one ad in one or two relatively low cost publications. If it works, you can build on your success gradually. That's how all of the great mail order successes started out.

Chapter

5

How to Add the Magic of Mail Order to Any Existing Business

"You only get out of it what you put into it. If you are a sheep in this world, you're not going to get much out of it." – Greg Norman

L et's say you already have a successful business. You either make some sort of product, or you are involved in retailing. You realize that there might be additional profit potential in selling through mail order.

By selling through mail order, you can reach far more people than you are able to at present, due to the limitation of your location or sales force. Maybe you're looking for a more economical way to reach your prospects. Or you would like to reach your present prospects with greater frequency.

One of the advantages of mail order is that you can reach people you have no practical way of reaching any other way. In retail or manufacturing operations, you concentrate your efforts on those people you think hold the greatest potential for you. This makes good sense, making best use of the resources you have at your fingertips. But you miss a lot of hidden potential this way. Mail order allows you to exploit this potential at an affordable cost. Mail order is the cheapest and most effective way to uncover this hidden potential.

And mail order is a great way to open new accounts. As you know, once you sell a person one item from your product line, he or she will be more responsive to buying other products from you.

PRODUCT MAIL ORDER

For a manufacturer who has a unique product he thinks has mail order potential, or for an individual who has access to such a product and would like to explore its mail order potential, it's relatively easy to find out whether the product can be a mail order success. Unfortunately, there is no crystal ball that you can look into and get the answer. After you've gained some experience, you will be able to make educated guesses as to what may work and what probably will not. But there is nobody on this green earth – in spite of what some mail order gurus might try to convince you – who can predict with absolute certainty which products will be successful and which will not.

However, there is a good substitute for the crystal ball. It's called "Testing". For a modest amount of money, you can make an advertising test of any offering whatsoever. This cost is the cost of advertising preparation and running a test ad. You do not have to tie up a lot of money on inventory. You do not have to set up an office, employ people, or develop an organization. If your venture proves initially successful, you can grow with it gradually as your needs require.

In preparing and placing an advertisement, it is important that you work through an established advertising agency that specializes in mail order direct marketing. They will guide you every step of the way, steer you clear of any of the pitfalls which could work to the detriment of the success of your offer. They will start off by giving you an opinion on the viability of your product, your pricing and your profit potential. This will give you an idea of what you might expect from a successful test.

One thing you should keep in mind is that if the offering does not test out well in the initial test, it probably never will. Accept the "verdict". Move on to something else. Don't delude yourself into thinking that a lot of tinkering is going to make a silk purse out of a sow's ear.

However, if results are borderline and you wish to pursue the possibilities, this is the time to work with your advertising agency in analyzing the results you received to determine if there are ways you might improve the appeal to get even better results. Of course, constant testing of new angles and fine tuning are the name of the game in mail order. Advertisers who have been using the same basic successful ads for 10, 15, 20 years or more and have a proven track record, still continue to fine tune through testing to see if there are things that they can do to improve their returns.

RETAIL MAIL ORDER

Items that are generally available in retail stores do not ordinarily make good mail order items. A store may advertise through catalogs and billing envelope stuffers to offer their present customers shop-at-home convenience. But for the most part there is no advantage in offering a product by direct mail.

Retailers use direct mail to build store traffic. Thanks to direct mail, the smaller store can compete toe-to-toe with the big retailers. It doesn't matter what size your store is or where it is located – the literature that is received through the mail carries virtually the same impact from the small retailer as from a larger retailer.

Summarizing some of the reasons a retailer may use direct mail:

1. To build traffic.

2. To announce promotions.

3. To maintain personal contact with their customers

4. To single out specific groups

5. To appeal directly to your competitors' customers.

HOW CAN A RETAILER USE DIRECT MAIL?

Billing Statement Stuffers. Sometimes the retailer prepares these statement stuffers himself. In other cases, manufacturers may supply these free or at very low cost.

Catalogs.

Catalogs allow the retailer to feature a number of different products, often tying in with a particular seasonal event such as Christmas or Easter, Mothers Day, Back-to-School, etc.

Customer letters.

A retailer may send out a letter for various purposes – to make an announcement, to keep in touch with customers for good will purposes, to attract new customers, or to reactivate old customers. These can be "Dear Customer" or "Dear Friend" generalized letters, or thanks to the advances in computerized laser printing techniques, these letters can be highly personalized to individuals, giving the appearance of a personally dictated and typewritten letter.

The retailer has a tremendous advantage in that he has a ready-made list of existing customers. Existing customers are always the most successful list for any direct mail promotion. These people are already "friends of the family".

In addition, it is possible to obtain very selective lists. For a small geographic area, sometimes the most effective approach is to use a geographic resident mailing. It is also possible to obtain lists from mailing houses with specific breakdowns, such as automobile owners, home owners, high income, interest in certain activities, etc.

There are many businesses that could easily add mail order to increase their profitability or add new clients or customers. A partial list includes:

• Law firms	• Doctors, Dentists, Chiropractors
• Automobile Dealerships	• Handymen
• Electricians	• Accounting Firms
• Air Conditioning & Heating	• Plumbing Contractors
• Residential Remodelers	• Commercial Banking
• Consumer Lending	• Insurance Agencies & Brokerages
• Financial Planners	• Investment Advice
• Real Estate Agents	• Automotive Repair
• Funeral Homes	• Retailers
• Nonprofits, Foundations	• Cultural institutions
• Hospitals	• Insurance companies
• Architects	• Engineers

- Hotels
- Associations

- Construction Companies
- Colleges

- Restaurants
- Health care

For a free, no obligation consultation, email superiorpress@sunmandirect.com.

Mail order can be a very easy way to add a new profit center to an existing business. It certainly should be explored. Most mail order agencies will not charge for an initial meeting to determine if a product or service can be sold through the mails. In a later chapter we will reveal how to find the right mail order agency for you.

Chapter

6

Secrets to Creating Winning Mail Order Ads and Direct Mail Packages

"When we can identify a problem and face the problem with confidence and enthusiasm, the solution is on the way." –
Zig Ziglar

One of the most important keys to success in mail order is good advertising copy. We talked earlier about the importance of having a good product to offer. Even more important than this is good copy. Good copy has more to do with the success of the offer than any other single factor!

Since it takes years of experience to become expert in the art of mail order copywriting, you are best advised to rely on the pros. However, it will be up to you to pass final judgment on copy, so you must be able to evaluate it. After all, no one knows what your product is and what it does better than you. And you have to pass final judgment on whether the copy conveys this properly, since it's your money that will be spent to advertise the product.

Therefore, here are some tips to help you evaluate good advertising copy.

There is an age-old formula which applies to all advertising, but particularly to mail order. It's known as **A I D A**. No, AIDA is not some Grandma Moses type little old lady with special hidden talents, or the name of a famous opera. Here's what these initials stand for:

A is for Attention. Your ad must capture the reader's attention instantly with an eye-catching headline. What we call a "stopper", a "grabber". Think about your own reading habits – when you skim through a newspaper or magazine, the first thing you do is glance at the headlines. If one captures your attention you will start reading the story. And you'll continue as long as the article holds your interest. It's the same way with advertising. Nobody reads every word in every publication from cover to cover. So you've got to grab your prospect and make him want to find out more about your offer.

I is for Interest. You have to build up interest in your offer by telling the reader what your product will do for them in terms they will understand and appreciate. We call this benefits. In order to do this, the copy must be exciting and convincing.

D is for Desire. You want to stimulate desire for your product or service. This is done by what we call "reason why". You show how the product or service provides the benefits that you have promised. You support your claims with documented proof, if it is available. A very effective way to support your claims is with testimonials from satisfied users.

A is for Action. You must ask your readers to do something. You must spur them to action. Every salesman is taught his first day on the job, "Ask for the order!" If you've convinced your prospects that they want your product or service, you want them to ACT. Now you may wish them to buy your product directly from the ad. Or you may want them to send in for additional free information – maybe the price is too high or too much additional information is required for the prospect to act intelligently on the spot. But it's important that you get him to do something. And do it immediately. Insist on urgency, don't let the reader put your offer aside with the intention of doing something about it later, because chances are he will forget about it or change his mind. That's why you see phrases like, "Act today!", "Limited offer!", "Don't put it off another day – tomorrow may be too late!"

The AIDA formula has been used for years and proven immensely effective. No matter how much experience you gain, no matter how expert you become, no matter what mail order tricks you learn in the future, you will always do well in evaluating your advertising copy by reviewing it against the AIDA formula.

WHAT TO TELL YOUR ADVERTISING AGENCY

O.K. You've got your product. You want to get the ball rolling and put it on the market. You're ready to talk to your advertising agency. We will tell you in Chapter Ten how to select an agency. But before you give your agency an assignment, you must do a little homework to get yourself prepared for the meeting.

FIRST:

- Write down the points about your product that you think your prospect will be interested in. Put them down on paper to help crystallize your own thinking.

- Assign priorities to these points. The ones you think are the most important.

- Start eliminating the least important points. Strive to determine which are the one, two, or three most important points – anything beyond that number can only be supporting points. After all, there is a limit to how much a reader can absorb or will stand for. Having too many points will only tend to confuse the reader and turn him off.

NOW GATHER SOME OTHER MATERIALS TO GIVE YOUR AGENCY:

- If you have used a sales pitch for the product, have it written out to give to the agency.

- If you have collected a file of advertisements for your product or competitive products, turn them over to the agency for review.

- Furnish the agency with a product spec sheet. If your product is something someone else manufactures, give the agency the manufacturer's spec sheet.

- Turn over all of the testimonial letters you may have from satisfied users.

- Let the agency know of any problems people have had with the product.

- Give them any publicity releases or published articles about the product.

- Let them have a sample of the product or photographs or a chance to examine and use the product.

Remember that the goal of mail order advertising is exactly the same as it is in any other form of selling; to get people interested in your product and get them to buy it.

The formula is different from knocking on doors or sitting across the desk from a buyer, or selling an automobile on a showroom floor, but the appeals you use are the same. You try to make the product so attractive that a person wants it and then make it really easy for them to buy it.

MAIL ORDER ADVERTISING IS SELLING. IT IS SALESMANSHIP IN PRINT.

HOW TO EVALUATE MAIL ORDER COPY

The agency will come back to you with a first copy draft. Plan on spending plenty of time together with them going over this first draft without interruption. Shut off the phones, if necessary, get out of the office.

There are two ways to judge copy. One is to go down a checklist. The other is to use your gut instinct about how you feel about the copy.

First, read the entire copy quickly to get a first impression. How does it strike you in general? If you basically like the copy, say so. If you don't, it's important that you say that, too. But be specific as to what you do not like about it.

If the copy meets this first test, then go back and check it against the AIDA formula: Does it grab your Attention? Does it pique your Interest? Does it develop Desire? Does it spur to Action?

How do you know when your advertising copy is finally ready for a test? Ask yourself these questions.

1. Have you got the most intriguing promise, a grabber, fact or pertinent question in the headline?

2. Does your copy elaborate on your claim? The text should immediately pick up on what you have said in the headline. Does the copy give "reasons why" this product is different or better than anything else on the market?

3. Put yourself in your reader's place: Are you convinced? Do you get excited enough about the product to say "Boy, I'd sure like to have one of those."

4. Does the copy back up your story with "proof"? Testimonials, product comparison tests, laboratory tests, etc.?

5. Does the ad ask the reader to take some kind of action? And does it make it easy for the person to act?

90% OF THE MAGIC OF A SUCCESSFUL MAIL ORDER AD IS THE HEADLINE

It is important to capture the attention of the reader, to get them to perk up their ears, as it were. This is the job of the headline. If the headline doesn't draw the reader into the ad, it doesn't matter what you say after this, because few are going to read it.

To grab your prospect with a headline, you must quickly offer something he wants or show them a benefit. What is a benefit? Something that answers these questions:

- What will the product do for me?
- How will the product improve my life?
- How will it make me happier?
- How will it save me time, effort or money?
- Appeal to the reader's self interest. Borrowing a philosophy from one of the greatest retailers of all times, Marshall Field, "Give the lady what she wants!"

Generally speaking, the shorter the headline the better. But it has to be long enough to make its point. Many people feel that the ideal headline is seven words or less. But, as Abraham Lincoln replied when asked how long should a man's legs be, he said, "Long enough to reach the ground".

A headline should be punchy, intriguing, interesting. A headline is more like a telegram than a conversation. Instead of saying "Here is a product that will end your foot pain", this whole thought can be wrapped up in three simple words: "End Foot Pain!"

HOW TO   People are always interested in how to do something. Using our same examples, we could use the headline "HOW TO end foot pain".

NOW   The use of the word Now in the headline adds a freshness, makes the reader feel that something can happen now that was not possible before. Using the same example: "NOW End Foot Pain" or "End Foot Pain NOW" promises the reader relief that they were unable to experience before.

FREE   This is one of the most potent words there is. The only hitch is that you really do have to give something free if you use the word. You may give something substantial such as "Buy one, get one FREE", or it may merely be "send for FREE catalog". The use of the word free is virtually guaranteed to improve response.

SICK/WELL   "First make 'em sick…and then make 'em well!" Bud Fisher, one of the giants in the mail order advertising business made this formula famous. You empathize with the reader and catch their eye by mentioning a specific problem. Then you make them well by offering a unique solution. This is a selective way of pin-pointing those particular people who would be interested in your product.

To use the same example on the painful feet, "If you suffer from sore, aching feet" (make 'em sick)…."end foot pain with Featherspring Foot Supports" (make 'em well). This is not only an excellent approach for the headline, but a good approach for the body copy of an ad as well.

You will note in this example that we included the name of the product. Although you cannot always work the name of the product into the headline, it is a good idea to do so when possible.

Be straightforward. Don't ever try to be cute or clever in a headline. This is too subtle. Too many people will not understand what you are doing and you will lose them completely. People are in a hurry when they are reading ads. They are not going to take the time to try to decipher what you have in mind. You will just lose them. There are very few cute or funny mail order ads that are successful. When you ask people to part with their money, it is serious business. It's no joking matter.

Massage your headline. In other words, don't be satisfied looking at just one headline version. Have the agency give you half a dozen headline alternatives. This way you can get a better feel for what you think the ad ought to say, you can compare the headlines against each other, and in the process probably find how to combine the best elements of several headlines to come up with one that's even better. Or looking at these headlines might stimulate an entirely different headline which is better than any of those presented.

THE BODY COPY FULFILLS THE PROMISE IN THE HEADLINE

The purpose of the headline is to get you going, to force you to read the first sentence of the copy. Then the first sentence must force you to read the second. Etc., etc., etc. The enthusiasm and intrigue should carry throughout the entire ad until you ask for the order and get the reader to act. If the ad gets dull or plodding at any point, the reader will turn the page, and you have lost the opportunity to sell him. That's one reason that good advertising copy is not simply written, but re-written, edited, honed, and punched up until every word sings like grand opera.

A good idea is to develop your own "swipe" file. Clip out mail order ads from newspapers and magazines which you think are effective. If you have seen a particular ad run repeatedly, this gives you a clue that the ad is working successfully. Study these ads. See what they have in common. This will start to give you a "feel" for good mail order copy.

And don't be afraid to copy or emulate successful mail order copy – obviously you can't pick things up word for word – but latch on to the common themes and ideas.

It's not necessary to re-invent the wheel in writing effective mail order copy. There are certain phrases and ideas that we see time and time again, but the reason we see them over and over again is that they work. Don't try to change them merely for the sake of change – only if there is a special reason for revising them. A good example is "Mail coupon today!" or "Send for FREE information today!" It says what you mean, it tells the reader exactly what you want them to do.

The "You" orientation. Always think in terms of what this product will do for "you", the prospect. Appeal to the reader's self interest. Talk as if you are addressing this one individual person alone. This does not always mean you have to use the word "You", but the implication must be there.

Many years ago Dr. Rudolph Flesch made a comprehensive study to come up with a way to measure readability. He determined two things about the printed word:

1. The longer the sentence is, the harder it is to read and the less the reader will get out of it.
2. The more short words, the more a reader will get out of it.

In other words, use simple words, use short sentences. And there are a few other things to look for in good copy: use the present tense whenever possible, use the active voice instead of the passive, use short-simple-punchy sentences, use connectors like "And", "But", "Plus", etc. to keep your copy flowing. And use more verbs than adjectives – verbs keep things moving, exciting, and flowing.

One final word about checking copy. Try reading the copy out loud. This is a great trick for finding out if there are awkward phrases, ambiguities, fuzzy thinking or verbose sentences.

Developing effective copy for advertisements applies to mailings as well – letters, catalogs, brochures, flyers, etc. When you have given final approval to the copy, there are several questions that have to be answered. How do you go about preparing and printing the materials? How do you get lists of people to send your package to? And how do you go about testing your advertising materials to increase their efficiency?

The first question we will answer is how to produce your mail order package – artwork preparation and printing.

HOW TO GET YOUR MAIL ORDER PROMOTION MATERIALS PRODUCED.

We talked about the copy before. Before any mail order advertisements or mailing piece can be produced, a corresponding layout has to be made, too. This is a rough drawing by an artist, which shows generally what the finished piece will look like – where the headlines will go, what they will say, how big they will be; the body type could be 'Greeked In', to simulate where the finished text will go; what the photography/illustrations will look like, where they will fit and how big they will be.

Copy and layout work as a team. When people talk about "the creative", they are referring to the copy and layout combination. Customarily in mail order, the copy is written first and then the layout is made to go with the copy. In some cases, such as catalogs in which a number of items are being sold, the layout may be prepared first and then the copy written to fit the layout.

There are two types of layouts: rough layouts and comps (comprehensive). A rough layout is, as its name implies, a simple rendering. It gives you a fairly good idea of how the finished piece will look. If you are a good visualizer, this will tell you enough to determine if you think it's on track. However, if you can't grasp what it will look like from a rough layout, you may prefer a comp. A comp layout is done with more meticulous care and comes as close to looking like the final printed piece as possible without actually being printed. A comp takes much longer to prepare, and you will have to pay more for it.

Once you have approved the copy and layout, a finished copy is prepared digitally for reproduction in a magazine, newspaper, or mailing piece.

Your advertising agency may have its own internal art staff and may also work with outside art studios and freelance layout artists who specialize in mail order. They are a special breed of artist, not so much oriented towards making "pretty pictures" and winning awards as they are in making high impact, sales-effective layouts.

If photography is required, your advertising agency will work with one or more independent professional photographers. Mail order photography is not something for amateurs. A professional photographer knows how to play up products and situations to the best advantage for selling your product. They also know how to photograph to bring out optimum quality in the final printed piece.

In some cases you will be able to save money by using stock photographs available from a number of stock photography suppliers. These are photos on file from previous commercial photo sessions, in which the models have already been paid and expenses amortized. This means you pay only a fraction of what you would have to pay for original photography.

But before you approve the ad, check it over thoroughly. Then double check it. Check for even the tiniest mistake. The time to make any corrections or changes is now! It is comparatively inexpensive to fix things at this stage. If you have to make any changes later, it will cost you dearly.

2- Typical Rough Layout

3-Digitally ready for reproduction

4 - Final piece as it appears in print

In checking, make sure the copy is in the right place, that the proofs are clean and crisp, that no copy is left out (sometimes "gremlins" misspell a word or cause the preparer to overlook a section of text, or position it in the wrong place).

Once you have given your final approval, it will be digitally transmitted for printing.

HOW TO ZERO IN ON YOUR PROSPECTS USING DIRECT MAIL

When you have your finished mail order creative package (including envelope, letter, brochure, order form, and return envelope) produced, you will want to mail it out to qualified prospects. This is where mailing lists come in. The big advantage of mail order is that you can target your market precisely.

The purpose of your list is to find potential buyers. You're looking for those who are most apt to buy what you're offering. Mailing list development and selection is one of the most important ingredients in any direct mail program. For your offer to be successful, you must reach qualified prospects for your product. Mailing list selection is vitally important – it can make or break you in direct mail.

Unfortunately the mailing list often becomes the weakest link in the mail order chain because mailing lists are taken for granted. The tendency is to get all caught up in the product itself and then the creative mailing material. The mailing list takes a back seat to the rest of the program.

Of course there's probably no such thing as a perfect list for any product. No matter what list or lists you choose or develop, there's going to be some waste. It's unavoidable. But what you do is seek lists that most closely match the type of people you think are the most apt to buy your product. The matching might be based on age, sex, geographic location, income, home ownership, interests and recreational activities, car ownership, size of family, education, occupation or any number of factors.

Basically, there are four types of lists:

1. Your own list.
2. Purchased or rented lists of people who have bought products that fit in the same category as yours.
3. Purchased or rented lists of people who have not bought your category of product, but have purchased similar products. For instance, someone who has purchased a camera would be a good prospect for a specialized photographic

print service. Or someone who purchased a personal computer is a prime prospect for computer software.

4. Purchased or rented lists of people who have not purchased anything in the category, but who have some personal characteristics that coincide with what you feel your most likely buyers would have.

If you're already in business, the best starting point is with your own list of existing customers. On top of this you will add all the prospects that you have called on. In addition, you'll refer to returned mail, sales call reports, shipping records, correspondence, and telephone inquiries. Also lists you obtain from your dealers or distributors. Finally, you might refer to association directories and trade show registrants.

One thing that is true of every list is that it is constantly changing. People move, change positions, retire, and they die. As a matter of fact, statistics show that one out of every three people change jobs, retire, or die every year. And within five years over half of all people in the United States will have a different home address. Amazing as it may seem, there is at least a 25% turnover in the average list every year.

If you don't keep up with the changes, you waste a considerable amount of money in mailing costs and the costs of printed materials. That's why it's important that you keep your own list active. You must establish within your own organization a system for keeping your list up to date. This cannot be hit-or-miss. It must be somebody's definite assigned responsibility.

In addition to your own list there are thousands of existing mailing lists available for you to buy or rent. These lists are generally available on a per-thousand cost basis. The rental of lists is for a one-time only use. One excellent source for locating appropriate lists is a publication put out by Standard Rate and Data Service called Direct Mail Lists Rates & Data. Your library may have a copy of this publication. It is a large volume and is published regularly. It breaks down available mailing lists into hundreds of different categories. For each list it gives a description and numerical breakdown of certain characteristics of the addressees…when, where, and how the list was developed…quantity and retail rates on a price per thousand basis and the minimum you can order…test arrangements…and how the list is kept up to date.

If you're dealing with a large list, do not mail the entire list to begin with. Select 5,000 names from the list for a test. If this proves successful, you can expand. If it does not, you have not spent a lot of money on something that isn't going to pay off.

List names and addresses can be furnished by the list suppliers on pressure sensitive labels, Cheshire labels (a form of label that can be easily affixed to an envelope with special equipment used by professional fulfillment houses), or by magnetic tape for computer addressing.

Be aware that list houses "seed" their lists to prevent unauthorized use. (If you rent a list for one time, don't think you can use it again on the QT without getting caught.) "Seeding" means planting a unique adaptation of a cooperating individual's name in a list so that they will notify the list supplier if they receive any unauthorized mailings. As an example, if a person's name is Jones, the seeded list might show him as "James" or "Jonus" to tip them off.

Rather than searching for your own list sources, you may call upon a list broker, an important specialist in the mail order field. A list broker is an independent agent who arranges the rental and addressing transaction between the list user and the list supplier. A list broker can save you time and effort, and often money. List brokers are listed in the same Standard Rate and Data Service Direct Mail List Rates & Data publication mentioned earlier. Here's how a list broker may help you:

1. Finds new lists for you.
2. Acts as one central source for all the list data you need.
3. Screens the information for you.
4. Reports on how particular lists have performed for others in the past.
5. Helps set up the list for valid testing in a split run.
6. Makes sure your instructions are followed by the list supplier.
7. Clears handling details with the list owner.
8. Checks the mechanical details of your mailing package with the list owner to avoid problems.
9. Works out the scheduling

In working with a list broker (or directly with a list suppler) give them some background information so they can help you as much as possible. Tell them what you are trying to do and why. Outline your goals. Give them an accurate and realistic time-table – don't play scheduling games.

And one final word, in selecting a mailing list. One of the most important things to know is that anyone who has bought something by mail in the past is a better prospect to buy something else by mail. They are the best prospects. Even better than this, somebody who's bought anything at all from you in the past, is more apt to buy something from you again in the future.

HOW TO TURN "SO-SO" INTO "STUPENDOUS"

Another one of the beauties of mail order is that it's so easy to test its effectiveness, revise it, and experiment to get a better payoff. With other forms of advertising, you don't know what is working and what isn't – advertising is just one element in the sales equation; if sales are up or down, it can be the result of any number of factors or all of them.

But with mail order, everything hinges on your advertisement or mailing package. There is no second guessing as to what is responsible for your success or failure. That makes it easy to compare one approach against another approach…through testing.

THERE ARE MANY THINGS YOU CAN TEST

1. The whole mailing package
2. The advertising copy
3. The price of the item
4. The offer itself
5. The lists you use
6. Individual pieces within the total package
7. Response devices

Before you do a test, spell out your objective first in clear simple language. What is it that you are trying to find out through the test? Is it your headline? Is it your copy approach? Is it your offer? Is it the pieces in the package?

The best way to test is through the split run. In the case of space advertising, there are many publications which permit you to split run your copy – which means that half of the publication's circulation will carry one version, and the other half will carry another version.

If you are mailing out a package, you can do a split run by mailing out two versions on an every-other-name basis.

Another way to test that's similar to the split run test, is to use what is called a Control. When you have used one advertisement or one mailing package enough to be able to predict what kind of response it will pull, you set this up as your Control. When you run a different ad or mailing, you compare the response against the Control. The new version could be identical to the Control, but with one variable such as a different price or different headline. Or it could be a totally different approach. When you find something that works better, that becomes your new standard to beat. And in a constant effort to improve, you can now test other variations against the new Control.

You will know which ad or package is pulling better by including a fictitious department number in the return address. You assign a different department number to every advertisement insertion or mailing. In a split run you use two different department numbers, for comparison purposes.

Here are some hints to guide you in mail order testing:

Test just one element at a time. Otherwise you won't know what causes different response rates. For instance, if you are testing a price of $12.95 vs. $19.95, don't change the headline at the same time. Or if you are testing one headline against another headline, don't change the price at the same time. You might think you can save time and money by combining two or three different tests at the same time, but it won't work. It will only confuse you and cloud the issue. If there are several things that you want to test, you're going to have to run several different tests.

1. Confine your testing to major items only, not every little detail.
2. Be sure your test covers enough people to give meaningful results.
3. Don't go overboard making big decisions based on little differences in results.
4. Don't try to read into your results factors which were not included in the test.
5. Don't expect your results to be the be-all and end-all.
6. Don't over test. And don't test just for the sake of testing. Testing is not a substitute for common sense, or a way to avoid making rational decisions on your own. It is a great tool to use to confirm your beliefs, or disprove them as the case may be.
7. If you don't think an idea is good to begin with, don't bother testing it.

But Never, Never, Never stop testing to improve your results!

Chapter

7

How to Know When You've Got a Winner

"A good advertisement is one which sells the product without drawing attention to itself." – David Ogilvy

The United States Post Office requires you to send and fulfill orders within a certain period of time.

If you want to build a successful mail order business then you should respond to your customer immediately after receiving an inquiry or order.

Imagine yourself, if you ordered or wanted information and took the time to write for it and had to wait a long time to get a response. Chances are you'd be likely to think twice before reordering or doing business again with the same company.

The same is true of refunds, or stolen, broken merchandise. Quick response builds credibility and credibility is very important in the mail order business. Remember it's not like dealing with the local store where you see the sales person face to face. When you're selling through the mails personal contact can be lost, so you need to do everything possible to encourage trust and satisfaction.

KEEPING RECORDS FOR RESULTS

Remember, your results are very important in determining the success of your business.

If it is inquiries you are tracking you'll need to determine the percentage of conversions. Those percentages are the guideposts for your determining whether an ad or mailing is successful.

All direct mailings and ads should be key coded and tracked. This not only allows you to determine the results of that particular test, but also allows you to test other elements within a partial test.

For example: Let's say you run an ad for free information on how to obtain details on getting free water (digging a well in your own back yard). So you key your coupon with AL0210 ("AL" for American Legion Magazine, "02" for February issue, "10" for 2010). But you want to test price on the water well. So you key your inquiries AL0210A for your regular price of $150 and AL0210B for the alternate price of $199.95 which you want to test. Then you can compare the response at each price level.

If 2,000 people respond to the ad keyed AL0210, 1,000 of them would get follow up material with AL0210A and 1,000 with AL0210B.

If 140 people order from AL0210A and only 100 order from AL0210B, then the "A" price per unit of $150 pulled a 14% sales rate, while the "B" price per unit of $199.95 pulled only a 10% sales rate. By keying the coupon and then the order form, you can see that the "B" version was still more profitable in the long run:

A/B Copy Test	"AL 0210A"	"AL 0210B"
Offer Price	$150	$199
Number sold	140	100
Gross Income	$21,000	$19,995
Expenses		
Ad cost	$6,595	$6,595
Cost of goods @ $50 unit	$7,000	$5,000
Net profit	$7,405	$8,400

In another example, the "A" version pulled in 140 orders, as in the example above, but the "B" version pulled in only 80 orders, an 8% sales rate. In this event, even though the profit per order was more for the "B" version, the final net profit to the advertiser was less.

A/B Copy Test	"AL 0210A"	"AL0210B"
Offer Price	$150	$199
Number sold	140	80
Gross Income	$21,000	$15,996
Expenses		
Ad cost	$6,595	$6,595
Cost of goods @ $50 unit	$7,000	$4,000
Net profit	$7,405	$5,401

HOW LONG WILL IT TAKE TO GET A RESPONSE?

When running an ad or sending a mailing piece it can take up to a year for the full life of the offer to come in. Some people report receiving results from a key code many years later. But don't worry, the bulk of the responses come within the first month.

This is the only scientific fact that holds true in the mail order business. It's called Double Day. For example, you run an ad in the May issue of American Legion Magazine and your first response comes in on Tuesday, May 5th.

If you count the total mail received from the first day until 30 mail order days later, you can take those figures and double them and that's what the ad will eventually do, even if it takes a year or longer.

The double day is different on space ads, depending upon the frequency of the publications:

- Daily Publications   5 days = double day
- Weekly Publications   10 days = double day
- Monthly Publications   20 days = double day
- Bi-Monthly Publications   30 days = double day

Direct mailings usually have a 10 day double day.

By using these double day figures you can quickly determine if an ad or mailing is going to be successful without having to wait a year.

KEEPING TRACK PHYSICALLY OF ALL THE MAIL

The first thing you need to do is devise a system that you are comfortable with and be prepared to modify, refine and change it over and over until you have it just the way you want it.

A system that works perfectly for one person may not be right for someone else.

The computer is a great tool and all successful Mail Order companies are online today. But here are some important pointers that work with or without a computer:

- Weigh your incoming mail. One pound of mail is equal to 100 envelopes. So if you are receiving orders at an average sale of $10.00, when your morning mail comes in, go to the mail scale and weigh it: 2 lbs = 200 orders = $2000.00

- Open the mail yourself in the beginning and you'll learn a great deal.

- Bank the money yourself. You can easily monitor deposits based on the average and weight scale.

- Mondays and Fridays are the busiest mail days, Tuesday the lightest.

- Assign a customer number to the order or inquiry so that you can build a file by number for easier tracking later.

- Fulfill immediately, especially if sending non-first class (i.e. bulk).

- Keep records of mailing dates to your customers so if someone writes and says they didn't receive, you can follow-up with knowledge, not speculation.

Timely response and accurate record keeping are the keys to handling inquiries and orders and most of all, building a satisfied customer base and a successful mail order business.

Chapter

8

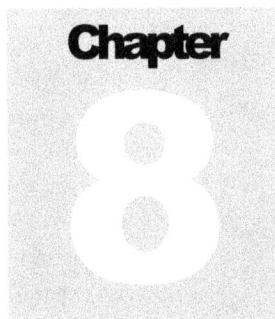

Sell From Your Ad or Your Follow-up?

"When dealing with people, remember you are not dealing with creatures of logic, but creatures of emotion." – Dale Carnegie

You usually think of mail order as where you present an offer to someone – either through advertising, by mail, or from a catalog – from which the customer orders the product directly from you through the mail, and you mail the item back to him or her through the mail. This simple, basic approach is what is called "one step" or direct sale.

Good examples of this approach would be when you see an ad in a newspaper or magazine or a message on TV offering a book or a CD or DVD or a small item, such as a wristwatch, article of clothing, specialized cosmetics, tools, telephones, health products, gadgets for your car, etc. The ad lists a price, and if it's in print includes a coupon, and asks the reader to send in a check or money order or allows the customer to charge the purchase to their credit or debit card.

But it is not always possible to sell an item in this basic one step manner. Sometimes it takes additional steps. Then the first step is designed merely to produce an inquiry expressing the prospect's interest in obtaining more information about the product or service. In response to this inquiry, a package of information is then mailed with some sort of ordering device. This gives the recipient an opportunity to learn much more about the product you are selling.

How do you decide whether to try to make your offer a one-step or two-step proposition? Well, there are several factors which ordinarily determine whether you will be more successful in selling one-step or whether you'll need a two-step procedure. The two primary factors are:

1. Price

A lower priced item (up to $19.95) can usually be handled as a direct one-step sale. People are less concerned about taking a "risk" on a lower priced item. One-step sales have even been made of items of $29.95, $39.95, $49.95...although this is less common. Generally speaking, the lower the price of the item, the greater its prospects for a successful one-step sale.

2. Complexity of the Offer

The second factor is the complexity of the product or offer and how difficult it is to explain what the product is or what it does. In an advertisement, it is very difficult to hold the reader's attention very long.

They've got other things on their mind. Consider your own reading habits. If you're like most people, when you read a newspaper or magazine, you skim over it as you flip through the pages. If a headline grabs your interest, you may start to read the article. But even then most of the time you will not read the entire article. This is even more true for advertising.

The longer, more detailed or confusing your message, the more apt people are going to flash past it, move along to something else. That's why your ad should be very long on promise, zeroing in on the end benefits, telling the reader why they would want to have what you are offering. If you are selling on a two-step basis, intrigue the reader, leave a little "mystery" to be solved in greater detail when they receive the packet of information they will send for.

TWO-STEP

A good example of this would be offering a home-study course in bookkeeping and accounting. The advertiser promises big job opportunities and part-time or full-time self-employment opportunities that await the prospect, the ease of getting into the field on your own, the vast size of the market, and how successful others have been as a result of taking advantage of this offer.

But there isn't time or space in the ad to go into details about everything the course covers, the easy financing plans available, how long the course will take, and how they go about taking tests and personalized instructor guidance they might receive, etc. Besides, going into too much detail in the ad may throw up too many questions in the prospect's mind, giving them too many reasons to say "no" before learning more about it. The most important thing you can do is whet the prospect's appetite, intrigue him or her enough to want to know more.

Another example of the two-step approach would be a program to interest a prospect into starting a business of their own, such as carpet cleaning, a fast food franchise, or automotive repair, where the expenditure could run into many thousands of dollars. Obviously you're not going to sell anybody directly on such a program without providing a great deal of detailed information.

In a case like this, your follow-up package might contain an enormous quantity of information. This information might normally include an exploration of the financial rewards possible, testimonials from satisfied customers, questions and answers, detailed descriptions of the product and/or processes involved, offers to talk to other users, guarantees that are available, financing, order blanks, etc.

Another reason for selling by the two-step method is to obtain hot prospect names for telemarketing follow-up

MULTI-STEP PROGRAMS

For some programs you might have multiple follow-up packages sent out over a period of time. Two, three or four separate follow-up mailings spaced weeks or months apart. Some successful mail order operators have used a series of as many as fifteen mailings.

There is no hard and fast rule as to how many follow-up mailings are proper. This is where testing and experimenting come into play. Obviously there is some expense to creating, preparing, producing and mailing out all of these packages. So the general rule of thumb is that you continue to mail out follow-up packages until on average, the additional returns from each mailing does not justify the cost to mail another package.

A word about how many items to include in the response mailing package: basically, "the more the merrier". Experience has taught mail order marketers that the more pieces you include in a mailing, the greater the sales you will achieve, as a general rule. A four-page letter will out-pull a two-page letter. But the longer letter must be very well written so as not to lose the attention of your prospect.

CONTINUITY PROGRAMS

There is another type of program called the continuity program. This is a program whereby the buyer signs up for a continuing program of product mailings. A good example would be a series of books, such as the Reader's Digest Book Club, or records, or jewelry ensembles. Basically the person signs up for the program and then on a periodic basis automatically receives follow-up product mailings for which they are then charged (customarily on VISA, MasterCard, American Express, Discover).

A common device is what is called the "negative option". You structure your offer in such a way that when a customer signs up they do not have to be re-solicited for every individual follow-up item. If you are in a "Mystery Book Club", you will automatically receive a new book to read every month or two. Once they start the program, the follow-up mailings are all automatic. Only if the person wishes to discontinue the program do they notify the company once they have signed up.

Customarily as an adjunct to this, the product carries a guarantee so that if the person receives it and decides at that point that he or she doesn't want it they may return it for credit or refund. Normally people do not return items. (If you get an inordinately high percentage of returns, it is usually an indication the product itself is faulty or unworthy, or a poor value for the money. Your problems can seldom be rectified through any change in your advertising message, if this is the case.)

A typical example is a jewelry continuity program whereby an offer is made for the prospect to receive a free ring, for example, which might have a retail value of $39.95 with a beautiful 1 carat cubic zirconium (man-made diamond) in a Sterling Silver or 14K Gold Setting.

In signing up to receive the free ring, the respondent is also signing up for the accompanying companion pieces, on the negative option basis. Thus when the ring is shipped to them, they also receive an announcement that within a period of time, say 30 or 60 days, they will receive matching earrings of comparable value, for which they will be charged.

If they choose not to receive the earrings, they will customarily get to keep the ring as originally offered, but they must send in a notification that they do not want the next item. Otherwise, 30 to 60 days later, they will receive the earrings, along with notification of the next item to be sent, possibly a matching necklace. And when they later receive the necklace, they will be told that the next item in the ensemble is a matching bracelet. Then when they receive the bracelet, the mailing will include an announcement that the final item in the package to be shipped is a brooch or pin.

SUMMARY

Mail order is not always a simple one-step proposition. If your offering is simple enough and the price is low enough, you may be able to sell directly from the advertising or mailing. Obviously this is more cost effective than going through the process of obtaining inquiries and then following up the inquiries with additional mailing(s) and/or telemarketing. But the decision as to whether to sell directly or embark on an inquiry-first-then-follow-up basis depends on the nature of your specific offer.

The astute direct marketer may test one approach against another if there is any question about which way to go. And in the end they may be satisfied with selling directly off the ad, even though they sell fewer units, if their resulting net profit is larger due to lower overall promotion expenses.

5 - A One Step Ad

This Bostonian Shoe ad does the complete selling job and asks for a direct order. The reader is asked to send in the coupon along with either check or money order, or permission to charge the purchase to his credit card. It is possible to sell directly off this ad because the product is simple in nature and can be adequately evaluated from the picture and description. Also the price is low enough that people will not feel they are risking major dollars.

6 - Step One in a Two-Step Program

Here is an example of an ad designed to produce inquiries only, rather than make a completed direct sale. The ad whets the reader's appetite for more information. Most inquiry producing ads feature a return coupon to make it easy to respond, and also to clearly spell out that the respondent is merely seeking information and not obligating himself in any way to buy. This particular ad tells the reader where to write for information, but does not have a coupon, simply because the ad is designed to look like a feature story, using what is called an "editorial format" – a coupon would nullify the "editorial" appearance of the ad.

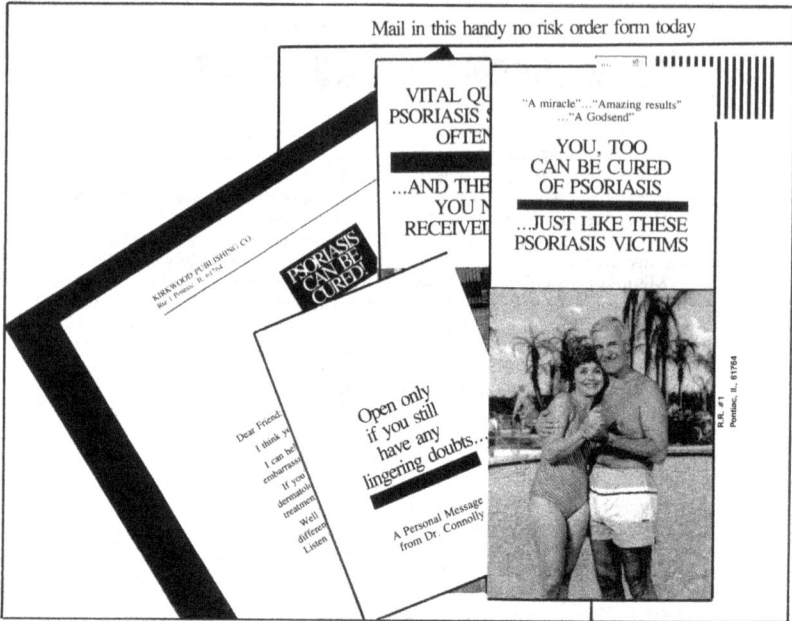

7 - Step Two in a Two-Step Program

Here is the packet of material mailed out to the prospect in response to his inquiry. This particular package is somewhat typical in that it includes a "teaser" envelope, a covering letter, a product/service brochure, a question-and-answer folder, testimonials and an order form with a pre-addressed return envelope.

SHOP at HOME SERVICE

A luxurious cubic zirconia ring free from Sears!

Please Accept a $29.99 Introductory Free Gift!

A Beautiful Solitaire Ring set with a magnificent 1 Carat Cubic Zirconia Imperial Counterfeit Diamond. Not even the skilled eye of some jewelers can tell it from a perfect genuine diamond and we're sending it to you FREE!

Dear Sears Shop at Home Customer:

This is truly a gift! You don't have to buy anything in order to receive it.

It's our way of introducing you to the Imperial Collection. So in order that you may judge the brilliance, clarity and perfection of our Cubic Zirconia Counterfeit Diamonds for yourself, we're sending you the elegant Ring, in your choice of size and finish, FREE.

Just sign and return the enclosed Postage-Paid "Introductory Gift Certificate," to indicate your choice of yellow or white gold and your ring size. Your exquisite Ring will be on its way to you promptly. (Use the enclosed 3-way Ring Sizer Card to determine your ring size.)

And Here's More Good News.

Your FREE Ring is part of the magnificent Collection of Imperial Cubic Zirconia Counterfeit Diamond Jewelry now being made available. The Collection will include a matching Pendant, Earrings, Bracelet and Fashion-Pin, each set with a full 1 Carat of Imperial Cubic Zirconia Counterfeit Diamonds.

By selecting the FREE Ring of your choice you will be enrolled in the program so you can decide whether or not you would be interested in examining the additional matching articles of Imperial Cubic Zirconia Jewelry.

When your Ring arrives you will receive an advance announcement advising you that the next piece in the Collection is ready for shipment. Then, if you do not want to see and examine the next matching piece from the Collection, simply return the Cancellation/Customer Service Card (enclosed with your Ring) to us within the 10 days provided, and it will not be shipped.

(over please)

However, if you are as impressed and delighted with your Ring as we are, if you agree that it is strikingly diamond-like, AND IF YOU WOULD LIKE TO SEE AND EXAMINE OTHER PIECES IN THE COLLECTION, THAT MATCH AND COMPLEMENT YOUR RING, YOU NEED DO NOTHING. As the matching Pendants, Earrings, Bracelet and Fashion-Pin are available, they will each be shipped to you for your examination about 45 days apart. You may cancel your examination privilege at any time.

As you receive each piece from the Collection, if for any reason you are not completely satisfied, simply return it and your account will be credited accordingly. If you decide to keep it, the Sears Shop at Home customer low price of only $29.99 plus $2.99 shipping and handling plus applicable sales tax will be charged to your SearsCharge Account (subject to approval).

We want to give you the opportunity to own and wear at least one of the magnificent pieces from the Imperial Cubic Zirconia Counterfeit Diamond Collection. Inspect it in the privacy of your own home, side by side with the finest diamonds you own. It is virtually indistinguishable from a blue-white perfect diamond.

Show your beautiful new Counterfeit Diamond Ring to your friends and family. Wear it unsuspected, side by side with perfect genuine diamonds. It bears such an amazing likeness to a gem quality diamond, it can only be described as "uncanny". We're positive you won't be able to tell them apart.

But remember: No matter what you decide, the exquisite Ring is yours to keep FREE from Sears Shop at Home Service (all you pay is $2.99 shipping and handling).

Here's All You Do:

Simply choose the Ring you prefer in rich 14 Karat Yellow Gold electroplate or radiant 14 Karat White Gold electroplate and use the enclosed 3-way Ring Sizer card to determine your ring size.

Then indicate your choice on the Postage-Paid "Introductory Gift Certificate" enclosed, sign it, and mail it to us today! We are delighted to send you this luxurious free gift.

Sincerely,

Janice Page
for Sears Shop at Home Service

P.S. Later on you will even receive news of an additional selection of magnificent Imperial Cubic Zirconia Jewelry items for both men and women.

SATISFACTION GUARANTEED OR YOUR MONEY BACK

8 - Continuity Program

This is the first letter in a typical continuity program. In this case it offers the reader a free cubic zirconium diamond ring just for enrolling in the program. Note the "negative option" feature of this program – matching jewelry items are mailed at regular intervals automatically, without any further action on the part of the respondent. However, the responder can drop out of the program at any time (even keeping the free ring if she cancels before the second item is shipped). Book clubs and record clubs operate on this same basis.

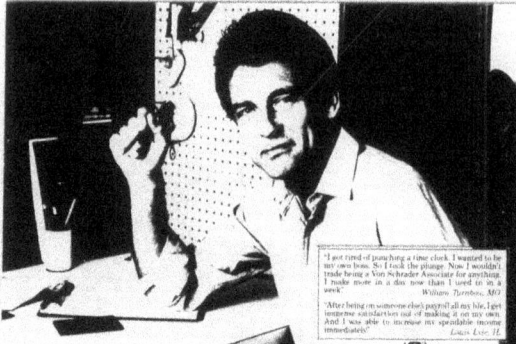

9 - Step One in Multi-Step Program

Here is a magazine ad directed at prospects interested in going into business for themselves. The details of the offering are far more than could be included in a single ad, and more than a reader would be apt to take the time to cover while reading a magazine or newspaper. Therefore, the coupon response merely indicates the prospect's interest in receiving more information.

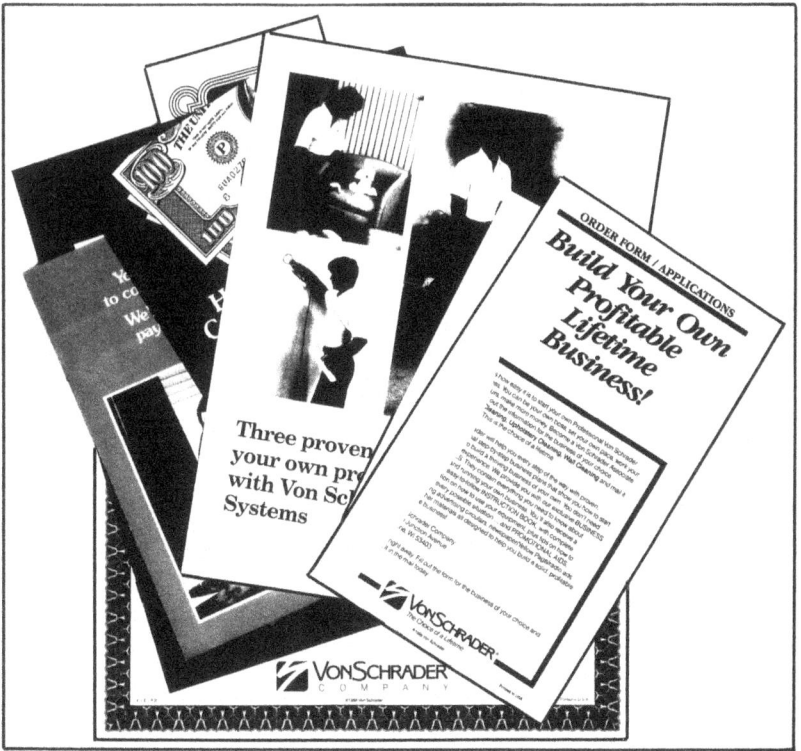

10 - Steps, Two, Three, Four, Etc.

In this case the prospect is being asked to make a major career decision, and spend sufficient money to make it a serious factor in his decision. It may take more selling effort for the prospect to make such a commitment than can be accomplished in just one follow-up mailing. Therefore, a series of additional mailings are sent out periodically.

Typically the "teaser" envelope and the covering letter change with each mailing. Some of the contents might be repeated in subsequent mailings, others might be replaced with different materials. The number of sales realized from each additional mailing helps determine how many follow-up mailings to make – eventually the mailings fail to bring in enough additional business to warrant continuation on a profitable basis.

Chapter

9

The Computer Makes Mail Order Easy!

"The good news about computers is that they do what you tell them to do. The bad news is that they do what you tell them to do." – Ted Nelson

Your Home PC, the greatest invention since sliced bread! It would be an understatement to say that the computer has revolutionized mail order. The computer has not changed the basics of mail order, such as Product, Pricing, and Promotion. But it allows us to do far more and do it faster and do it with less effort. It speeds up all of the mail order processes and it permits us to have far more intelligent information at our fingertips with which to make decisions. Decisions which can spell the difference between success and failure, moderate success and phenomenal success.

It is not necessary to have sophisticated or expensive computers. A simple home computer will work wonders when you are starting out.

There are seven major uses for the computer in mail order:

1. Developing and planning your program
2. Developing and maintaining mail lists, keeping them up to date, using them in mailings.
3. For personalizing standard letters and other documents.
4. To process orders and inquires you receive.
5. To analyze your market, sales and other responses.
6. For desktop publishing.
7. For bookkeeping and business operations.

PROGRAM PLANNING

As you accumulate data or obtain available information from outside sources, you can use this information to zero-in on the audience you should reach for maximum profitable results. Your computer can speed up the whole process, from giving birth to an idea through the development of the particular program and getting your offer in front of your prospects.

Computers have made list selection more productive. With the additional information the computer age has brought to individual names on each list, you can be more specific in selecting the people to whom you present your offer – not only by age, sex, occupation and general location, but by such things as hobbies, home ownership, vacation habits, mail order buying habits, etc.

By using such information in selecting your mailing lists, you can increase the number of responses per dollar spent. Or to put it another way, you can hit the same sales goals while spending less money.

MAILING LISTS

There are two types of computerized lists. Those you can rent from outside sources, known as "list houses". And lists you develop yourself.

Usually the most productive lists are the lists you develop yourself from previous customers. They know you. They know your product. They are the best candidates for re-ordering it, either for themselves if it is a product that gets used up, or for duplicate products to be used as gifts for family and friends. Furthermore, if you are like most mail order operators, as you add products to your line, they are apt to be companion products, products in the same general family. For example, if your first offering was a scratching post for cats, additional products might include a cat bed, kitty litter, vitamin food supplements for cats, etc. Obviously, anyone who bought your first offering is a cat lover, and thus is in the market for other cat products.

Many times you will receive names from different sources and some names will be duplicated. It costs money to mail out duplicate materials needlessly. Therefore you can merge or combine the names from several different sources…and at the same time you purge or eliminate duplicates.

For lower cost bulk mailing rates, which is what most mail order advertisers use, the post office insists that your materials be sorted by zip code. The computer is indispensable for combining and breaking down the names by zip codes. As a matter of fact, the computer can combine lists in a number of different ways. Ordinarily we think of having names listed alphabetically. But the computer can take the same basic lists and sort it out not only by zip codes, but you can customize lists by income, education, sex, age, city, state, population density, home ownership, telephone or automobile ownership, pet ownership, just about any factor you think would be of interest.

Once you have built up your own list of sufficient size, this list can be an added source of income for your mail order business. Many people don't think of it, or aren't aware of it, but your lists may be highly prized by a lot of other mail order companies. This is because if people bought from you by mail, chances are they will buy from others by mail. Particularly mail order businesses who are looking for the same type of customers that you have. So you can "rent" your list to others. This probably answers a question that you've often asked yourself when you receive certain catalogs or letters in the mail; "Where in the world did they get my name?" Chances are you bought something through the mail from somebody at some time, which got you on somebody's list, and they rented their list to others.

There are all kinds of lists available for rent. What the term "rent" means is that the list supplier will furnish you with printed labels or allow you to borrow a computer tape of a particular list on a one-time, single use basis.

COMPUTERIZED LETTERS

You've undoubtedly received letters that were sent to you that seemed as if they were written personally to you. The greeting contained your name. The letter was addressed personally to you as "Dear John" or "Dear Mr. and Mrs. Smith". Even in the body of the letter it may have said things that personalized the letter even further, chatting about "your friends and neighbors on Elm Street" or "all the dog owners in Center City". These little devices are inserted to make it seem like a highly personal letter rather than a general mailing sent to "Dear Friend". Experience has shown that personalized letters get more attention than general ones.

There are two types of personalized computer letters – one is where the entire letter is typed out by computer; the other is where the contents of the letter are pre-printed to look like typing, then the personalized information is individually filled-in by computer. This second type is not quite as effective as the first, but sometimes it is the only practical way to go from the standpoint of time and money.

When you get into quantities like 50,000 or 100,000 copies or more, the time and money saved by going to a "fill-in" letter is important enough to go this route. But for most quantities you will be interested in, at least until you get well established, you're probably well advised to use fully-typed letters.

Computerized letters combine the basic letter you have written with computerized mailing lists. The computer takes the two sources and automatically integrates them, so that virtually all you or the mailing house needs to do is put the information in and push a button. Obviously a computerized letter is more expensive than a totally pre-printed "Dear Friend" letter. The decision on which way to go depends a great deal on whether you think the computerized approach is worth the extra expense. Generally speaking, the higher the price of what you are offering, the greater the desirability of the computerized letter. Also in mailing charitable donation appeals, the personalized letter is far more effective.

PROCESS ORDERS AND INQUIRIES

Processing orders is more than just cashing the checks and mailing out your product. You must produce a label and keep a record of what you sent out and when you sent it. By using a computer you are forming a permanent record of the customer. This becomes part of your own mailing list, which you can use in the future to send out companion product announcements, special offers, catalogs, etc. It has often been said that the real money you make in mail order doesn't come from the first sale...but is derived from your own personal "captive" customer list, from additional sales. The names and addresses you store in your computer are like gold!

In a sense, processing inquiries is even more of an effort than processing orders. With an order, you produce a label, slap it on a package, and put it in the mail. With an inquiry you have to send out a package of follow-up material. Then you have to keep track of whether you receive an order in response to the follow-up package. Possibly send out one of more additional follow-up packages periodically. You've got to establish some kind of automatic system that keeps track of your follow-up efforts, and what results you get from them.

ANALYZING YOUR MARKET AND SALES RESULTS

In its simplest form, you can look at your mail order efforts merely as making an offer through an advertisement or a mailing, and then taking in the orders and money and sending out your product in response to every order you receive. The trouble with this approach is that you'll never learn anything operating this way. You'll never learn how to improve your results. You'll never find out how to make more money to put in the bank for every dollar you spend – and after all, that's what being in the mail order business is all about!

That's where your computer becomes invaluable for you. Information can be broken down by inquiries and sales. You want answers to questions like the following; How many inquiries and direct sales did you get from an ad run in any particular publication? Or from a selected mailing? How and when did your prospect respond to each inquiry? How many of these inquiries were you able to convert into actual sales? What did each sale cost you in relation to the cost of running the ad?

This information is vital to your future success. It will tell you such things as which publications work best for you and which ones are unproductive. What are the best audiences for you to set your sights on reaching? What times of the year bring you the best requests? How many follow-up mailings are worthwhile to send to your inquirer?

Such information can help you qualify the leads you get. It costs as much to chase a bad lead as it does a good one.

BUSINESS OPERATIONS

You can use your computer for billing purposes, for correspondence, for doing your bookkeeping – things like accounts payable, accounts receivable, inventory, petty cash; to generate income statements, balance sheets, cash flow projections, and so forth.

But with your computer you can do much more!...

Every day you face tough business questions that are vital to your profitability, your ability to grow, or to simply make a go of it. It's important that you have the tools at your fingertips to make the right decisions. Simple software programs can put an expert business planner right by your side to show you how to analyze those tough questions and lead you to the right answers.

Your computer can guide you through the development of a professional plan on how to go about getting financing, and to develop marketing strategies. It will ask you all the right questions and lead you step-by-step in developing a feasibility plan, business plan, marketing plan, financial plan and contingency plan.

Moreover, it will help you prepare complete financial projections, budgets and analyses., producing many different kinds of reports for many different uses.

As a helping hand in your day-to-day operations, your computer will help free up time from repetitive accounting tasks so you can concentrate on running your business efficiently and making profits. It will reduce paper clutter and keep the mess off your desk. It will provide you with "to-do" lists and deadlines.

In addition, your computer and printer will produce professional-looking labels and quickly and easily design and create all the forms you'll ever need; contracts, applications, shipping forms, purchase orders, expense reports, statements, invoices, message pads. It'll even fill out business forms with speed and ease.

Best of all, computer business programs that are available today are designed for people who know nothing about accounting and bookkeeping. You don't have to be a computer genius.

DESKTOP PUBLISHING

The electronic publishing revolution has rewritten the book on preparing mail order materials for printing and advertising. New machines and software are bringing print shop quality type and graphics to everyone.

A scanner can convert pictures and art to digital form. A few simple commands size the illustrations, add headlines, body copy, coupons, call-outs, captions…and in a few minutes a laser printer cranks out camera-ready originals for your print shop to duplicate.

It used to be you'd have to pay an artist and typesetter $1,000, maybe $2,000 or more to prepare a mail order flyer. Now you can do it yourself with the right software and your personal computer

Inexpensive PC-based electronic publishing systems make it economical for even the smallest mail order business to create ads, flyers, brochures, labels, instructions, whatever you need.

SUMMARY

The computer has opened great new avenues to the mail order marketer. It is an invaluable tool that will help you develop and plan your programs….to create effective mailing lists…to personalize mail order letters...to process your inquiries and orders...to study your market and analyze your sales response...to produce camera-ready materials for printing and advertising...and finally, to streamline all operating aspects of your business.

Chapter

10

How to Select the Right Mail Order Advertising Agency

"One secret of success in life is for a man to be ready for his opportunity when it comes." – Benjamin Disraeli

Selecting the right advertising agency at an early point in your mail order business will save you many thousands of dollars in wasted testing and hundreds of hours of time.

An experienced mail order advertising agency will show you many short cuts to success.

They will know the right publications or lists to test. They will have access to the best mail order rates. They will produce ads designed to present your product properly to the public so that sales can be produced at a profit.

The right mail order advertising agency should be considered your partner in every meaning of the word.

Their goal is to make sure your every effort is profitable to you because only then will you be willing to commit even greater expenditures insuring more profits to you.

HOW ADVERTISING AGENCIES MAKE THEIR MONEY

Most mail order advertising agencies work on a commission basis. Generally that commission totals 15% of your media expenditures.

For example, if you run an ad in a magazine that costs you $1,000, the agency would receive $150 – not from you, the advertiser, but directly from the publication.

If your advertising budget grew to $100,000, the agency would receive $15,000. So you can readily see that an agency has a vested interest in your success. The more dollars you spend, the more income they receive.

In addition to the commission, an agency will charge for other services. These other services could include:

- Copywriting
- Layouts
- Production of ads

These charges are almost always quoted in advance, and vary depending on the time necessary to produce the work. Some agencies prefer to charge on a fee basis for all their services and this is usually on a negotiated hourly rate.

Now that you are more aware of what an advertising agency does and how they charge for their services, you're better prepared to evaluate individual agencies and find the one that's best for you.

WHERE TO FIND AN AGENCY

Mail Order Advertising Agencies are very specialized and may not necessarily be found in your city.

Major metropolitan centers such as New York, Chicago, Los Angeles, etc., all have a few of these specialized agencies, but location should not be a factor in your decision.

With overnight mail delivery, telephones, fax machines and the Internet, where an agency is should be of little importance to you. What you want to evaluate is their ability to produce good work in a timely fashion.

Many of the most successful mail order companies have their advertising produced thousands of miles away because they have learned that the most important reason for choosing one mail order agency over another is their track record.

HOW SUCCESSFUL HAVE THEY BEEN FOR OTHER MAIL ORDER COMPANIES

The chances are excellent that an agency that has successfully sold knives and watches and jewelry by mail could also sell cosmetics and health aids and fashion by mail and you'll find that most successful mail order agencies have clients selling a wide variety of products.

A good mail order advertising agency will not only produce ads that return profits to you, but as your partner they will help price your products for maximum profitability.

They will make sure your ads are placed in the proper publications. Further, they will negotiate the lowest rates to assure the highest profits.

They will also be a constant source of new ideas on how to make your advertising dollars work harder and smarter.

TAKE THE RIGHT STEPS IN BECOMING A MAIL ORDER EXPERT

The first step in selecting a mail order agency, is for *you* to become a "mail order expert". This is easier than it sounds because one becomes expert in mail order by becoming a student of mail order ads and publications.

Read the mail order magazines. Go to your local newsstand or supermarket or, if necessary, to your library where you can get the names and addresses of mail order publications and subscribe to them.

A partial listing of successful mail order publications would include:

- National Enquirer
- American Profile
- Parade
- U.S.A. Weekend

- Popular Science
- Grit
- Popular Mechanics
- Elks
- V.F.W.
- American Legion

These are just a few of the hundreds of magazines that run mail order ads on a consistent basis.

You'll need more than one issue of each magazine because you're going to have to make a list of ads (both classified and display) and determine which ones appear regularly.

Those that appear on a regular basis do so because they're profitable to the advertiser.

Contact a few of these regular advertisers and ask to speak to one of the principals.

You'll find that mail order people will be glad to share information and most will volunteer the name of their agency.

The most successful mail order advertisers have their accounts with a handful of specialized mail order advertising agencies.

Another source to find a good mail order agency is the publications themselves.

By calling some of the magazines and speaking with the salesperson who handles mail order, you'll be given the names of who they consider to be the best agencies they call on.

Where the agency is located should not enter into your decision – you should only be concerned about their ability to produce and place profitable ads.

Once you've narrowed down your search to one or two agencies, just ring them up, ask for the president or another senior member of the company and tell them forthrightly about your product and desire to succeed in mail order.

You will want to know about their successes with other advertisers and how they charge.

In most cases it's not necessary to meet in person.

Once you're convinced you've found the right one, you'll need to send them a sample of your product, your cost in the mail and how much you intend to charge.

The rest is up to them.

If you had confidence in choosing them, then have confidence their ads and media tests will work.

That doesn't mean you can't have input in copy and layout, but if you want things changed, do so for good reasons. If you allow your agency to do what they do best, you're well on your way to mail order success. It's important for you to share the results of tests with your agency so they can evaluate their efforts and, if necessary, make changes so your ads do even better the next time they run.

CHECKLIST IN SELECTING THE RIGHT AGENCY

To sum up, here's a 10 point list to help you select the right mail order advertising agency for your new mail order business.

1. Read the mail order magazines – become a student of mail order.

2. Make a list of those advertisers whose ads continue to run, week after week, month after month.

3. Call a few of these advertisers and ask the name of their agency.

4. Contact the publications and ask them the names of those mail order agencies they work with.

5. Call the agencies and ask about their successes. Many will even be glad to give you names and phone numbers of their clients for you to call on your own.

6. Determine how long their best clients have been with them. Longevity = Success

7. Get the name of the specific person who will be responsible for your account. Even though you may be small potatoes now, you're entitled to work with the best people so you can become one of their major accounts.

8. After making your decision, treat the agency as your partner – hold nothing back. The more they know about your product, the better job they will be able to do.

9. Give them the freedom to do their own thing. You've hired them to write your ads and make your layouts. Don't second guess them or "nitpick" words. Make changes only for good reasons.

10. Share your results. Tell them what's working and what's not and then allow them to make changes so that your next test does even better than your first.

Chapter

11

The Internet – Super Charging your Mail Order Business

"The Internet will become profitable. It's an old story played before by canals, railroads and automobiles" – Paul Samuelsonhe

The Internet is a revolutionary force that continues to evolve. If you are not using the Internet in your mail order business then you are missing out on the marketplace to the world.

Having a brick and mortar business no longer means that you only cater to local residents. The Internet has made it possible for you to bring in business from an online source, and that can be very lucrative.

You may not be familiar with online advertising and find it a bit intimidating. That's normal, but you'll find after reading this chapter that it's not hard to do on your own, it doesn't cost much (if anything), and it's a quick way to increase your revenue as well as branding and exposure.

Maybe you've tried your hand at building your own website, but it never quite got off the ground. Your site traffic was weak and you gave up, believing this whole Internet thing was just hyped up without merit.

First, it's important that you wipe the slate clean and look at online promotions through a whole new perspective. There are many reasons why it's vital to any business to have an online presence – even if it's a local service that you provide and no one across the country would be popping in to pay for it.

There are three main reasons why you need an online presence.

CUSTOMERS NOW PRE-SHOP ONLINE

Consumers don't just get in their car and drive around town to find what they need. And they don't let their fingers do the walking in the yellow pages anymore. Instead, they turn to the Internet to do some pre-shopping and once they narrow it down, they buy from the best retailer available.

That could mean they buy from somewhere locally, or have an item shipped from as far as overseas. But finding the product or service isn't even the sole reason that prospective customers go online, either.

They're looking for more information than who happens to carry an item in stock or provide a service.

Now, it's possible to get feedback and details about products and services before you ever invest a single penny.

Many online shopping sites now contain consumer reviews. This is far more powerful than seeing a blatant advertisement by a company. A customer buys a product or pays for a service, goes online and not only rates it on a scale of 1-5 (or 1-10), but also leaves detailed feedback on what they liked, or what they hated about it.

Any entrepreneur can say he has the best product on the market, but it's what the customers say that holds true. It's great to have an area where your customers can share their testimonials and vouch for the quality you provide.

Another item of interest in the pre-shopping routine is simply gathering more information. Instead of picking up a product in a store, you can get questions answered online from the manufacturer, retailer, or a consumer who once had the same question and is now sharing the answer with others!

IT EXPANDS YOUR SELLING AREA

Services usually need to be handled locally, but products can be bought and sold from anywhere in the world. When you use an online store, you're no longer relegated to the corner market.

Geography ceases to be an issue with an Internet presence. It doesn't matter if the product you sell is tangible or digital, you can reach a global audience just by putting your products for sale on the 'net.

As an offline business owner, you probably know the expensive advertising costs associated with reaching your demographic. A billboard can drain your ad budget in less than one month.

Newspaper ads in big cities cost an arm and a leg, making small business marketing virtually impossible for the print media world. But taken to the World Wide Web, suddenly the playing field is level – you have just as much chance of capturing the business of an interested prospect as a Fortune 500 business owner.

IT ALLOWS YOU TO TEST VARIOUS ASPECTS OF YOUR BUSINESS

All businesses – on or offline – do a bit of testing to see what works best in getting potential customers in the door and converting them into paying customers. Online, you can have cold, hard statistics to analyze – eliminating the guesswork of why someone came to your store (or how) and what the result was.

You can't track a person driving in his or her car down a highway from the moment they see your sign and walk up and ask them how they got there as soon as they enter your store, following them around to see if they wind up buying anything.

Well, you could, but they'd probably feel weird being tracked like that – and it would be impossible for you to track every single visitor to your storefront. Online, though, it's completely possible to see where someone made the decision to visit, how long they stayed, what path they took through your virtual storefront, where they decided to leave with or without buying, and many other aspects.

There are four main things you can test online to help you nail down the marketing plan that will best help your bottom line for profitability.

BRANDING

How do you want your business to be known? In a physical store, you have one chance to make a first impression. But online, you have the opportunity to brand yourself several ways.

Regardless of whether you sell products or services, you want to showcase your expertise. With the Internet, you could test several variations of one home page and see what type of branding resonates best with your target audience.

BENEFITS

What makes your customer whip out his or her wallet and pay you for a product or service? There might be a whole laundry list of things, but it's hard to pinpoint in a physical storefront.

Online, though – you can swap out the list of benefits or showcase them all and see which perks your prospects respond best to. Then what you do is replicate your online efforts in your physical store and see if sales increase from it.

PRICE POINTS

In the brick and mortar store, you can run sales, but you can't sell a product to one person for one price and another person at another price. Online though, you can set up multiple storefronts and get crucial feedback on which price point help you make more sales.

In the same day, you might have 10 people buying your product at $17, 132 people paying $37 and 78 willing to spend $57. Your research will nail down the best price point (in this case $37), and you can then set your in-store prices accordingly.

PACKAGES

Sometimes we pair items together to make them more attractive. A good example would be spa services or a gift basket of items. Online, you can devise a store shopping cart that lets consumers pick and choose, and you'll be able to determine which packages would be the best fit for your in-house customers as well as online ones.

The best thing about all of this testing and tracking is that you can tweak your sales in an instant, not wasting any time to switch out what works better for what wasn't working well at all.

It's important to know how to establish a strong online presence, now that you know why. You don't have to spend a small fortune to do it, and you can be up and running quickly.

How to Establish an Online Presence

Knowing that you need an online presence is one thing – knowing how to get one is what confuses most small business owners. They've heard that it takes upwards of $10,000 to have a company site built, and the do it yourself attempt didn't work out, so they feel stuck.

There are four main things you need to know about when building your piece of virtual real estate on the World Wide Web – how to get a domain and hosting, what site pages you need to get started, how to set up a company blog, and what you need to do to optimize your site so that it gets found by your customers.

DOMAIN AND HOSTING

Some small business owners go online and sign up with a free service who allows them to build a page on their own site. This isn't the same as having your own site. It's just a page, and that means you're not in control.

A domain name is the URL or location of your online business. It begins with a http://www and ends with a .com or sometimes a .net or .org (to name a few).

You want to buy a domain that your business owns from a site like GoDaddy.com. Don't buy all of the bells and whistles that go along with it – just the domain. It's better to get site building tools and hosting elsewhere.

You can choose a domain one of two ways – it's a personal choice that's up to you. First, you can simply register your business name. There's just one problem there. Let's say you own the domain in California – but someone in Florida has the same business name.

Only one of you can own the domain name on the Internet. When you begin looking to build your online business, you might be disappointed to learn that someone else already owns yourbusinessname.com.

If this happens, and you still know that you want to own your business name as the URL, then you can simply change the ending of the domain. If they own dot com, then you can try to register the dot net or dot org versions.

Another way to go about it is to hyphenate the business name. If they already own bestflowersever.com and that's also your company name, then you can register best-flowers-ever.com and use the hyphenated version.

When you register your company name, you're not always making it easy for people to find you. For example, let's say I live in New Hampshire and I'm trying to find the best bakery.

Your bakery is named Everything's Creamy. Well if I don't know the name of your business already, chances are those aren't the two words I'll type into a search engine like Google to find a bakery.

You have to think like a prospective customer. They would probably type in "best New Hampshire bakery" or something along those lines. So this is the second method you can use to choose a domain name, if you don't go with the name of your business.

This is known as a keyword phrase – a word or group of words that are relevant to your product or service. How do you find the keywords to choose from? Go to Google's own keyword tool here: https://adwords.google.com/select/KeywordToolEx ternal and type in the broadest keyword for your niche market.

If you own a bakery, you'd type in bakery. The keyword phrase you choose for your domain might depend on whether you actually sell products or services to online buyers or if you're only building an online presence for local customers.

So for instance, if you could grab NewHampshireBakery.com that might be perfect –

unless you plan to sell baked goods that can be shipped worldwide. Then you might want to choose a keyword phrase that works better for that purpose, such as onlinebakery.com or bakerydeliveries.com.

Once you find a keyword phrase that looks like it gets a good amount of searches per month, you'll plug it into GoDaddy to see if it's available. Using our examples, I find that NewHampshireBakery.com is available and could be mine for just $10.69 per year.

The other two are taken, so if you wanted something that would work for a wider market, you'd need to go down your keyword list and see what phrases are available as domain names.

Next you'll need to get a hosting account. The host is what keeps all of your files activated for you so that your site is live. It's important to sign up with a reputable hosting company, because you don't want your site to have much down time (which could result in lost revenue).

Perhaps the best-known hosting company used by online entrepreneurs is HostGator. It's very easy for newbies to use, and they have a 24/7 365-day Live Chat or phone-based help desk where someone can assist you if you get confused or encounter a technical issue.

With HostGator, you can get a plan for as little as $4.95 per month. If you plan on only having one site, then this is your best option. But once you build more than one site, you'll want to upgrade to the Baby plan for $7.95 per month.

Once you have a domain and hosting, you'll log into GoDaddy and go to domain manager. Put a checkmark next to the domain you just bought and click the NameServers option. Choose the last option that says, "I have specific nameservers for my domains."

This is where you'll enter your HostGator Nameservers. You can find those when you log into HostGator – in the left sidebar, near the bottom of the page. There will be two of them and they'll look something like this:

NS485.hostgator.com

NS486.hostgator.com

Paste those codes into GoDaddy and save.

Back in HostGator, click the AddOn Domains button and enter the information about the new domain there. Now you're ready to start uploading files to make your site go live on the Internet!

MAIN SITE PAGES

Now you're on to site design and page building. You don't want anything busy or garish looking. A business website is clean and professional in nature. If you don't want to use a site builder yourself, then you might want to look at portfolios of freelance web designers on Elance.com or RentaCoder.com to hire a freelance professional and get competitive bids.

Most companies need a few specific pages to get them started.

THE HOME PAGE

This page is where people will most likely enter your site (but not always). You want to share a little bit about what your business is, what you sell, and why it's so great. The Home Page is also where you'll want to put an opt in area.

We'll talk more about this later in this chapter, but basically, you'll be building a list of subscribers so that you can email them any time – with special deals, news, or product information. It's not spamming because it's all based on permission.

THE ABOUT US PAGE

A more in-depth description of the business and its employees can go here. You might give a company history, talk about the press you've received, and let the prospective customer get a feel for who you are.

THE FAQ PAGE

Customers always have questions. This is a good place to compile them along with their answers. You can add to this over time. It might be something as simple as, "Do you ship overseas?" to something more specific like, "Do any of your products contain peanuts?"

THE PRODUCTS OR SERVICES PAGE

Products and services may have just one page – or quite a few. You can include a thumbnail picture of the product (that expands when they click on it) and a description and price. You'll need to work with your web developer on what type of shopping cart you plan to use (PayPal or something else), so it will have an order button, too.

THE ORDER PAGE

If you're offering services, then you might have a package page that describes the items, and a separate order page where the visitor ticks off what they want and completes the process with an order.

If you have many items and pages, then the shopping cart solution will allow the user to place items into a virtual "cart" and then check out when they're finished.

THE TESTIMONIALS PAGE

Once you begin accumulating feedback from your customers, put it online and let others see what good things have been said about you and your company! Make sure you have permission to use the testimonial before doing so.

You may also want to have a feedback form so that people can submit these to you automatically. Then you choose which ones to post, and which ones to respond to privately.

THE CONTACT US PAGE

Whenever someone lands on your website, there's nothing more frustrating than having a question and not seeing any way to reach you. You should have a contact page that includes the physical address of the store, mailing address (if different), phone number, and email address.

You can also have the web developer create a contact form that gets submitted and automatically sent to you.

Company Blog

It's very easy to create a blog using HostGator and a domain of your own. Log into HostGator and click on Fantastico De Luxe. It's a smiley face button. In the left sidebar, under Blogs, choose WordPress.

Then click New Installation. You can install a blog right on the home page of your site, but if you're a brick and mortar business, you'll probably want a regular Home Page and a separate blog page.

It will ask you to choose the domain from a drop down list. It then asks you where you want to install the blog. Under "Install in Directory" you can enter the word blog. This will place your blog here:

www.YourCompanyDomain.com/blog

Give yourself an administrative username and password and set your email address before clicking Install. You'll be taken to a page where it asks you to double check the information before clicking Finish Installation.

The last page shows you where your log-in will be, and you can then go there and log in to start blogging for your company. What do you blog about? Remember that keyword tool?

That's the perfect place to start. Keywords are how your site will be found. So let's stick with the same example. If I go back to the Google keyword tool and type in online bakery, I see a few keyword phrases that I can build blog posts about.

Start with the highest search volume and work your way down.

If the keyword phrase is … buy cake … then your blog entry could be called … Buy Cake Online and

Ship to Your Home ... or ... Buy Cake Online as the Perfect Gift!

Then you simply write a short 250-word (approximately) article using that keyword phrase once or twice and publish it. When Google comes to visit your site to see what it's about, they'll see these keywords being used and the next time someone types in buy cake, your site might be one of the top ones presented to the person searching, giving you the opportunity to make a sale!

It's best to blog on a regular schedule, but here's what's great about blogging – you can queue up blog posts to automatically publish for you! You can outsource the writing (at Elance.com for instance), and just paste the article into your blog, and set a publishing date for it.

Some small business owners even get the freelancer to do this task for them, too. You can set up a publisher login for them and have them write the post and set a publish date – so that you're hands-off, only checking to make sure the articles read well and represent your company in a good light.

The Importance of SEO

SEO is Search Engine Optimization. There are whole books on SEO and companies whose job it is to do nothing more than SEO your site. But don't let that intimidate you. You can do some of it yourself, and later if you want to improve your ranking in Google, you can hire a professional to analyze it if you wish.

Choosing a keyword-relevant domain is the first step in good SEO practices. Using keyword phrases in your blog content is another. You want to make sure the web developer you hire knows good SEO practices, too.

The page should load quickly and it shouldn't have any broken links or obstacles for Google's search engine robots. These are also known as spiders – they crawl the web looking at sites and figuring out how to rank and categorize them.

You can't stuff too many keywords into your site or Google will think you're doing something shady like spamming people. Place a keyword phrase in your title and page header (your site builder will ask for this).

Start building backlinks to your site. We'll talk about pulling in free targeted traffic later, and that will help some, but for SEO purposes, you can contact other relevant sites and ask for a link exchange – you carry a link to their site and they do the same for you.

In Google's webmaster tool section here: www.google.com/webmasters/tools, you can build a sitemap so that when Google's spiders reach your site, they know how to access all of the pages and index them so they can be presented to people who use Google to find information.

If your web developer tried to get you to pay a lot for some fancy Flash program, you might avoid it. It can be a detriment to your search engine optimization and some people who land on your site won't have a flash player.

Provide plenty of content on your site. With too few words, Google won't know what your site is about. That's where a blog comes in handy. You'll have ample content with keyword usage to help them figure it out.

Maintain Communication With Your Prospects And Customers

Communicating with your customers is a wonderful part of having an online business. In a brick and mortar store, once the customer leaves, you really don't communicate with them again until they come back.

Or, you snail mail them coupons or store announcements, but mailing costs can be expensive when you have a large list of customers. Online, you have the ability to build a list of both prospects and buyers – and email them on a schedule or whenever the need strikes you.

This form of communication is called email autoresponders. You build a list of data that includes your prospect's name and email address, and they give you permission to contact them via email.

The system has what's known as a double opt in, which means the user signs up once and then your system emails them a notice saying they have to confirm their subscription. This is to prevent people from having others maliciously sign them up for emails without their consent – and it offers a bit of protection for you from being labeled a spammer because you then have proof that the subscriber asked to be contacted.

CHOICES FOR EMAIL COMMUNICATIONS

There are many email autoresponder systems on the market, but there are three main ones you can choose from. They range from free to paid, but like most things, the free versions are limited and the paid versions more reliable.

MAILCHIMP

MailChimp is a free autoresponder system that some small business owners use to get started. This should only be an option if you have zero dollars to invest in your list building, because one day you'll want to upgrade and it won't be a piece of cake to do it unless you stick with the same company.

With a free autoresponder system like this, you're limited in the amount of subscribers you can sign up (500) and the number of emails you can send out each month (3,000). Later, if you want to upgrade on MailChimp, you can pay anywhere from $15 to $690 per month and up depending on the size of your list.

GETRESPONSE

GetResponse is widely used by many small business entrepreneurs who promote products online. They have some very cool features – like text to voice email, where your subscribers can listen to your email message while doing other things.

They also have video email marketing, so the messages you send can actually play a video message of you talking to your customers. This personalizes your messages and helps brand your business better.

AWEBER

Aweber is the most well-known and respected autoresponder system. For a little less than $20 per month, you can have unlimited lists and send unlimited emails out to your subscribers. Their pricing goes up to $130 monthly for 25,000 subscribers and you can contact them for bigger lists.

HOW TO SET UP AN OPT IN FORM ON A SQUEEZE PAGE

When you start building a list of customers, you want to have a dedicated page set up for your opt-in form. You can also put small opt in areas on other portions of your website, like your blog sidebar.

A squeeze page is not a full sales page. You don't show all of your products there or tell about the company. A squeeze page has a headline, maybe a sub-headline, and a few bullet points about what you're going to be giving away on your list, or the reason they'll want to sign up to it.

You might give away a short free guide, or promise to email them with special offers, sales information, or advice. Give them a reason to exchange their personal contact information with you, because that takes a lot of trust.

Once you sign up for an account (we'll use Aweber as our example), you'll log in and click Create a List. You're going to give the list a name and description and enter your return email address and name, so it shows where the email is coming from.

You can include some company branding details here too, like your company name, website URL, logo and a signature that goes out on all of your email communications automatically.

At this point it will enable you to connect your Aweber account with your social networking site pages, like Twitter or Facebook. And you can choose whether or not you want to get an email notification every time a new subscriber signs up to your list.

On the next page, you can personalize the confirmation email that goes out to people who have signed up. Now it's time to grab your web form code.

If you're creating the site yourself, save this code in a Txt file. If you're letting someone else build it, copy and paste the code to them so they can create your squeeze page.

You want to click Web Forms, and then Create a Web Form. You can split test two different web forms to see which one works best, if you want to. On the web form, you'll choose a design.

They have over 400 design templates you can choose from. It will default with you asking them to enter their name and email address only. But you have the option of asking for more information by clicking on Create a New Field.

For instance, you can enter Phone Number to get that information, too. You can add other elements to your web form, like a counter to show how many people have seen your opt in page.

Save the web form and then click on Go to Step 2 where you'll give the form a name, save it and click to get the code. It will give you three options for code. The first will give you the HTML or JavaScript code that you'll cut and paste into your web file.

The second will send an email to your web designer containing the HTML and instructions they need. And the last one will allow Aweber to host the form for you, and you'll link to the page from there.

MANAGING YOUR EMAIL COMMUNICATIONS

Emailing your customers must be done with care. They've entrusted their contact information to you, so it would not be wise for you to start spamming them several times a day.

Some business owners do email their subscribers daily, but you'll have to find the number that best suits your style and the desires of your subscribers. If you notice people are unsubscribing in droves and telling you it's because you email too much, then you might try cutting back.

There are two types of emails you can use with an autoresponder system – the follow up and the broadcast. Both have good uses, and it's best if you use them in conjunction with one another.

FOLLOW UP

Follow up emails are great because you can queue them up in the system and they get automatically sent out to your readers on a timeline of your choosing. So for example, you could write five emails tonight and schedule them to go out once a week for the next five weeks.

Follow up emails should be informative in nature, but you can also do some selling in them, too. Many online business owners queue up a whole year's worth of emails to help communicate with their subscribers on autopilot for them.

BROADCAST

A broadcast email gets blasted out to your subscribers once. This is perfect when you have a sudden sale that you need to let people know about or you want to poll them for an upcoming event.

BASIC EMAIL TIPS

There are some basic email etiquette and strategy tips that can help your communications convert into more sales for your business. Here are a few top tips online entrepreneurs use regularly:

Your email titles should be clear. Let the recipient know what the email message is about. And don't trick them into thinking it's about one thing, when it's really another. If they're giving your email attention, don't break their trust by tricking them.

Offer tips and advice on how to make the most of using your product or service. This could be the opt-in offer that you present on your squeeze page. You might help with the technical setup of your product or offer tips to enhance their experience.

Don't use complex email message designs. Most entrepreneurs keep it simple by using regular text emails. Some people won't go to the trouble of fixing their settings to view any HTML code but you can test both types on your subscribers and see what works best!

Get personal with your subscribers. Yes, you're there to sell things to your recipients, but that doesn't mean you have to be all business all of the time. Let your subscribers build a relationship with you by sharing some simple information – even something as simple as what you did on your family vacation the previous week, tying the story in with your product or business in some way.

Track the responses of your email campaigns. Your email autoresponder service will likely have some tracking elements built into it. This way, you can tell how many emails bounced due to bad email addresses, how many people opened their emails, how many deleted them sight unseen, and how many unsubscribed because of the message. Adjust your messages once you see the results of your tracking efforts.

Email marketing is a standard part of doing business (or just promoting) online. Don't be afraid to start building your list. You can even have a list of prospective customers that automatically transfers them over to a buyer's list once they invest in your products or services, so your initial follow up emails are helping them make a buying decision and the secondary list ensures they stay satisfied!

Pulling in Targeted Free Traffic

Let's talk about what targeted traffic means, because you're going to hear other online business owners talking about this. Targeted traffic means that you're bringing in your perfect audience to your website – someone who would readily buy your product or pay for your service.

Non-targeted traffic is anyone who happens to land on your domain, whether or not they'd be a potential buyer for you. So an example might be a dog training site – your targeted audience would be a dog owner whose pet is posing problems for them.

A non-targeted visitor would be someone who happened to click through on a link but they don't have a dog, may not ever have a dog, and you're not sure why they're there in the first place. Maybe they were looking for cartoons about Snoopy and your site mentioned a puppy named Snoopy, so Google provided your link to them.

There are ways you can help bring in targeted traffic to your site. There are paid methods and free methods. We'll talk about paid methods next, but it's important to do as much free promotion as possible because that way you keep advertising costs down.

ARTICLE DIRECTORIES

Article directories are a great way to bring in visitors who are interested in your products or services. The great thing is, they let you provide some expertise and information and link back to your own website so the reader can learn more.

What's even better is that your articles go viral. Viral marketing is when you do some sort of advertising and others spread it for you for free. So with article marketing, you would write an article about your niche, post it on a directory, and allow publishers to pick it up and use it.

Here's the catch – they can use your content, but they have to keep everything intact. Your name is still the author, and your links are still live. This means others who have websites or email lists in the same niche can help promote you – all because they need some content.

Before I teach you how to use article marketing from a writing standpoint, I want to mention one other way you can use them. You can pick up someone else's article as a publisher, post it on your blog, and use it for search engine fodder.

Google will crawl your blog and see that it's relevant content and help index your site better for people who use that search engine. Now you do have to abide by the rules and keep everything intact, but you can also write an introduction to the article and a conclusion, adding your own links too.

HERE'S AN EXAMPLE OF HOW YOU DO THAT:

Introduction: From time to time I like to share great resources that I find with my own blog users. While researching the latest dog training tactics, I came across a wonderful article I wanted my readers to see. I'll post it below and then add my own insight to it afterwards.

[here's where you insert the article that you found]

Conclusion: As you can imagine, this is great information for dog owners! I found a wonderful resource to help you implement this dog training strategy and in the coming days I'll talk more about this product and its pros and cons. In the meantime, check it out here [insert link] because I think this is really going to change the way we train our puppies from this point on.

As a small business owner, you may not be accustomed to writing articles. Don't be intimidated if you feel you don't have any writing talent. There are plenty of freelance individuals who you can outsource to and you retain 100% of the rights to use the articles under your own name.

If you want to outsource, go to Elance.com or RentaCoder.com and post a project for someone to write you some articles that are at least 400 words each (some directories require even longer articles, such as 600 words).

Expect to pay anywhere from $5 to $30 per article. Most times, you get what you pay for, and a decent article will be about $10 per page. But sometimes newcomers to Elance will charge rock bottom prices just to get a few projects under their belt so they have feedback.

Look at their portfolio to see what their writing style is like. And you can look on the article directories to see what types of content is written and published on these. Remember the keyword research we talked about previously?

Well those same words and phrases are what you'll develop your articles around. So if your keyword phrase is "beauty supplies," then you'll develop a title for your article such as, "What's the Difference Between Organic Beauty Supplies and Non-Organic?" As long as the keyword phrase is used in order in the title, that's fine.

I'll give you a list of the top 50 article directories soon but let's talk about one example on how to use it so that you know the basic protocol. The most popular one is Ezine Articles.

On EzineArticles.com, you'll be allowed to register for a free author account. That gives you ten article submissions at first. EZA is basically testing you during this phase. They want to know if you'll submit spammy articles, if you'll try to pass off plagiarized content, etc. So be on your best behavior.

Once you have the 10 articles passed, they may give you another 10 tries (if they had to ask you for a lot of revisions) or, they could just give you Platinum author status immediately if they love the quality of your work. This means you get articles approved faster (48 hours as opposed to a week), and you can submit unlimited articles to their directory.

Have your article pre-written, and then log into the system and click Submit New Article. Here, you'll pick the best category for your content, give it a title, short description, and paste your article in.

It will allow you to hyperlink back to your site after the first few paragraphs, and you can include a resource (author's) bio box with links, but make sure you read their rules and guidelines before doing anything because they often change and you want to submit it without any problems.

Once the article is approved and live, you'll be able to use it on your own blog. Plus, you can log into your dashboard at any time and see how many other publishers have picked it up and how many times it's been found in the search engines.

The stats for your articles will tell you how many views it has had, how many times your URL was clicked, and what that click through rate is (percentage-wise). It can also tell you how many comments it has, and its rating if someone has rated it.

This is handy information to have because then you'll know what's working best and duplicate those types of articles for your different directory accounts. You can even point your freelance writers in the direction of those articles so they're aware of what's working best for you.

Here are the article directories I promised below – and make sure you try them all out (if applicable) so that you know which ones work best for your business:

1. www.ezinearticles.com
2. www.articlesbase.com
3. www.suite101.com

4. www.buzzle.com
5. www.articlesnatch.com
6. www.helium.com
7. www.goarticles.com
8. www.articlealley.com
9. www.articledashboard.com
10. www.ideamarketers.com
11. www.selfgrowth.com
12. www.amazines.com
13. www.bukisa.com
14. www.articlerich.com
15. www.articlecity.com
16. www.searchwarp.com
17. www.isnare.com
18. www.sooperarticles.com
19. www.articleclick.com
20. www.a1articles.com
21. www.articlecube.com
22. www.infobarrel.com
23. www.submityourarticle.com
24. www.web-source.net
25. www.articlecompilation.com
26. www.365articles.com
27. www.site-reference.com
28. www.abcarticledirectory.com
29. www.articlestars.com
30. www.EvanCarmichael.com
31. www.articlepool.com
32. www.articlenexus.com
33. www.articlesfactory.com
34. www.articleslash.net
35. www.articlewarehouse.com
36. www.carolinaarticles.com
37. www.upublish.info
38. www.article-buzz.com
39. www.acmearticles.com
40. www.thewhir.com

41. www.e-articles.info
42. www.articlecell.com
43. www.affsphere.com
44. www.articlebliss.com
45. www.thecontentcorner.com
46. www.articlemonkeys.com
47. www.articles.everyquery.com
48. www.dime-co.com
49. www.articlewheel.com
50. www.ultimatearticledirectory.com

Social Networking Sites

Social networking sites are sites where people share ideas, information, and tactics and people interact with those who share them! There are so many social networking sites – with more being launched each day – that it's hard to tell you about them all, so I'll give you the big three and you can use Google to find more in your niche.

SQUIDOO

Squidoo was built by an entrepreneur who wanted a place where "Everyone's an Expert." That means he wants you to share your expertise with the world, and he gives you a very easy platform to do it on.

You don't need to know how to build a website. You just use his built in system to register a page on Squidoo and then add content to it through the use of various modules. So for example, you would again use your keyword list to register the page like this:

Squidoo.com/organicbeautysupplies

The organic beauty supplies portion in bold is the area that you type in. Then it takes you to a page where you can add modules. Modules are like building blocks. So you might add a text module for some written content, then a video module if you have a YouTube video, and maybe a poll module if you want to poll your visitors.

There's no limit on the amount of modules that you can add. But they are wary about spammers using their system so make sure you read the rules about what topics they don't allow.

FACEBOOK

Facebook is the largest and most used social networking service; at the time of this writing it has just surpassed 500 million users. The Facebook terms of service require that users give their true identity and declare they are over the age of thirteen. Users create a profile that includes personal interests, activities, philosophy, education, work and much more. Users can also join common interest user groups organized by characteristics like workplace, school, college, favorite movies, television shows, bands and more. Users then add their friends and family and can exchange messages, share photos and spend a great deal of time socializing.

For marketers a great free feature is Facebook pages. Pages allow businesses to broadcast information in an official, public manner to people who choose to connect with them. Pages can be enhanced with applications that help you communicate and engage with your audience, and capture new audiences through friend recommendations, News Feed stories, Facebook events, and more.

A new or existing business should use pages as another channel for reaching your potential audience.

When you see a Facebook reference in a print or television ad or as a link on a website they are typically pointing to a business Facebook page. Due to the enormous size of the Facebook audience every business should have a Facebook page. You will need to promote your page with a link from your website as well as making your audience aware of this page through all your other marketing communications. The object of promoting your Facebook page is to get Facebook users to like your page. When a user "likes" you, they are in reality saying they want to become a member of your Facebook community. As a member they will receive your page posts in their Facebook news feed and if you allow the ability able to comment and respond to on your posts.

You can promote your Facebook page through paid Facebook advertising, which is very similar to Google ad words. Facebook ads are small unobtrusive text and small images that are displayed down the left hand column of the Facebook page. The ads are so low profile that some Facebook users may not even be aware that these links are paid advertising.

Since Facebooks knows almost every thing about their users the ad platform gives you an amazing amount of options for targeting your Facebook ads. You have the usual demographic and geographic information but you can also micro target using other Facebook attributes such as belonging to specific groups. The options are numerous and constantly evolving. However in the beginning you can keep it simple and free by using your Facebook page as an extension of your blog. If you have a good technical resource they will be able to connect your blog to your Facebook page, so when you make a new blog post it automatically pushes a status update to your Facebook page. A simple strategy for getting results from your

Facebook page is to post short duration specials or discounts. These are basically digital coupons that can entice your fans to take an action such as ordering a product or requesting more information.

TWITTER

Twitter is a social media service of a different stripe. Twitter allows you to communicate short – very short messages – 140 characters in length. The background for this limit is the mobile phone revolution and the limit of SMS (Short Message Service). The object was to be able to get out the crux of you message. Millions of people are having these mini conversations on any conceivable subject. From the Twitter web site or the various 3rd party Twitter applications you'll want to see what other people are interested in so we can make connections by following those folks and publishing what you are interested in thus getting other folks to follow you. It's about relationship building.

Twitter is also described as a micro-blog. It may not seem that this format grants enough room to state anything worthwhile. But in fact, the reality is this micro-blog format keeps you from running on and on and forces you to be laser focused with the key idea you wish to convey. These short messages are the perfect digestible size for the new world of faster interactions and shorter attention spans.

The savvy marketer can use this service to pop off a quick promotional note to the community with an web link to send folks for more details or to ask them to take some kind of action.

Your messages are known as a "tweet". Sometimes it's just a general Tweet of seemingly minimal interest such as, "I'm scheduling a meeting with a possible retailer." Sounds like you're just talking about your day, but it's branding you as being someone who makes something happen – someone to listen to. At other times, it's a question to the crowd: "What do you look for on a website before you order and what will immediately make you leave?" Sounds like you're just chit chatting, but you can use these interactions to research your market for your next promotional test or landing page test or as fodder for a blog post.

Due to the message length limit of your tweets you'll want to learn to use a URL shorting services like TinyURL. When you're tweeting about your newest product, you have to keep the news within 140 characters. This can be challenging if you have a huge URL in your message. TinyURL takes that super-long URL and turns it into a tiny one - one that will fit into a tweet very neatly. TinyURL also helps avoid broken URLs or mistakes if they are accidently written down incorrectly. One other feature is that TinyURL hides the ultimate destination of the URL from the user - which can be helpful when you redirect to an affiliate site.

The current trend is to use Twitter as a means to let the public get to feel like they know you. Because once they do - once they're your followers and "friends," they'll feel comfortable paying for your products or services.

We like learning that someone we follow is traveling to New York. We like hearing he's attending a Broadway show. It makes them more touchable - more real than just a brand name. You may not think your life is as exciting, but just being a real person is how to build trust with your audience. Marketer's today need to establish a connection with prospects before tapping them as customer.

LINKEDIN

LinkedIn is the social networking site used mainly for professional and business networking. At this time, Linkedin is reporting 100 million users with about half their members residing in the United States.

Members use the site to maintain a list of contact details of people with whom they have some kind of professional relationship. A contact network is built up of direct connections, the connections of each of their connections and also the connections of second-degree connections. These can be used to gain an introduction to someone a person wishes to know through a mutual contact. Every day people are using this network to find jobs, people and business opportunities recommended by someone they know from their contact network. The "gated approach" is intended to build trust among the members.

LinkedIn also allows companies pages. Small and large companies: AT&T Business Solutions, Dell, JetBlue, Juniper Networks, Liberty Mutual Insurance, Microsoft Corporation, Philips, Squarespace, and StrongMail, have Linkedin company pages for promoting their products and services. To create a LinkedIn company page you must have access to your company's domain name, typically the email address is based on this domain name for example - @yourcompanyname.com is the domain name for "Your Company". If you are a young company and you don't yet own your domain name, you'll want to explore LinkedIn groups as a vehicle for promoting your company.

Once you have your company page, you'll need to enhance your profile by requesting recommendations or testimonials from your clients and customers. As more LinkedIn members comment favorably on your business, you'll be using the network affect to reach new potential customers through these credible recommendations.

When a Linkedin member searches for your company, will they find an active company profile with many good recommendations or will they see a company that doesn't participate in the new media spaces. The cost for these efforts can be low, but they are not zero and at the very least they do require time for constant feeding and maintenance. What you put forth inside the network tends to be what you get out.

LinkedIn also supports the formation of interest groups, and at the time of this writing there are some 870,000 groups whose membership varies from 1 to 200,000+. These large groups are employment related, but you will find a wide range of topics around professional and career issues. If you do not have the ability to create a company profile page, and you have determined that the Linkedin professional audience is a good target, then you need to create a group that you can use to promote your product or service

Groups support a limited form of discussion that is moderated by the group owner. Groups can be private, accessible to members only or may be read by any Internet user. After you create the group, you can grow it organically by sending compelling promotional messages that ask others to join your group. You can also look at other Linkedin discussions and post comments and ideas, make sure that on any posts you include your signature and make sure it includes links to your profile or group.

HUB PAGES

Hub Pages is very similar to Squidoo and about equally effective. You register a Hub page using a relevant keyword just as you do on Squidoo. You use the same type of page building blocks to add content to the page.

Hub Pages is a little stricter on some things. For example, Squidoo allows nine links per page, but Hub Pages only allows two. They both have some spam topics that they steer clear of, but that's only because a few bad apples spoiled it for everyone.

GOOGLE KNOL

Google Knol is a bit different in that it's almost like an article directory that you can add images and hyperlinks to. It doesn't really have page building blocks like Squidoo or Hub Pages.

A Knol is a unit of knowledge, so each page you create should represent a snippet of knowledge you want to share about your topic. Try not to make these social networking pages sales letters – you have your own website to sell on.

What you want to do is write informative content about the niche as a whole. So if you sell a line of skincare products, you don't want to openly sell it on social networking sites. Instead, you want to share knowledge about skin disorders, like psoriasis, acne, organic product measures, and more.

FORUM MARKETING

Forum marketing (sometimes known as a bulletin board) is when you go to online forums and join and participate as an expert in your field. Your expertise can be as simple as answering questions others have asked. Each forum has different types of marketing opportunities.

We'll highlight three of the top methods you can use:

SIGNATURE FILE

A signature file (commonly known as a sig file) is a bit of text that automatically posts under each response or post you make in an online forum. It's like an automated signature instead of you having to sign your name each time, but it delivers some awesome marketing potential, depending on the forum and their rules.

Instead of just signing your name only, you can post a hyperlink (again, depending on the forum rules), and drive traffic to your domain. Signature files work really well when you're showcasing your expertise because people will be impressed with your posts and click through on your links to see what else they can learn from you.

BUILT IN FORUM BLOG

Some forums allow members to claim their own blog. This helps you generate more traffic and many will allow multiple hyperlinks within the blog, too. The key to blogging on a forum is to keep selling to a minimum and provide lots of good content.

You should blog on a forum blog the same way you blog on your own domain – by using keyword-relevant titles and posting frequently.

ADVERTISING SECTION

If you're lucky, the niche forum will have an advertising section for you to post in. Now some will charge you a fee, but some will let you post ads for free, and you should take advantage of this opportunity.

In these ad sections that are dedicated to selling, it's perfectly acceptable for you to write a mini sales page for your post, complete with colorful headlines, bullet points, and even image screen shots if applicable.

While free, targeted traffic is wonderful, it does take a bit of time to build on. In the meantime, I'm going to teach you some paid traffic methods that help you get potential buyers onto your site in minutes, but you need to be careful that you track your spending and profits from these strategies.

Securing Traffic with Paid Measures

Sometimes you don't want to wait for a free traffic method to take root and grow into something wonderful – you want results right away. But rushing into paid advertising can mean you make costly mistakes, so make sure you know what you're doing first.

There are a couple of ways to pay for targeted traffic to your website. The two most prominent ones are Pay Per Click (PPC) advertising and buying ad space for your promotions.

PAY PER CLICK ADVERTISING

Pay per click advertising is when you have an ad listed somewhere and you only pay whenever someone clicks through on the ad to go to your website. You'd think that would mean you'd always make more than you pay, but that's not always the case.

Most online entrepreneurs use Google AdWords as their pay per click search engine of choice, although there are others you can use, too. With AdWords, you'll set up an account name and verify it, as well as set up a billing system before you can begin running ads.

Once set up, you can create a campaign! First you'll choose your campaign settings. That means you'll choose where the audience is located and in what language you want to advertise in.

You'll also choose where you want ads to appear – just on Google's search engine, or their partner sites, too. And Google will ask you to set a budget for your campaign per day.

Set this low, because Google will help you spend that amount per day if possible. Some people set it high, and quickly realize their mistake when the ads were clicked on, but they converted into very few buyers.

One of the perks of running a PPC campaign is that you can test your sales pages to see what converts best. Remember, you can increase your budget at any time, so test the waters carefully before jumping in.

Google will want you to set a Cost Per Click number (a minimum of $0.01). This is how much maximum you're willing to pay for each click. That doesn't mean you're going to pay that amount! You could pay much less, but when it comes to competition, they need to know how far you're willing to go.

Bids help Google figure out what position your ad receives, but that's not the only determining factor, so don't go into this thinking you can outbid someone for a #1 position.

Once the settings are complete, you'll need to set up an Ad. You can see what the ad will look like. You get room for a headline, two description lines, a display URL and the real destination URL.

The headline should be using a keyword or phrase, because whenever the user types that word or phrase into Google, Google will automatically bold it, so that it stands out more.

The two description lines can detail some perks of using your product or service, or it can tell a little about them.

The display URL is a clean way of showing people where they're going, such as www.website.com, while the destination URL is the real URL. So let's say website.com is a complete site about dog training.

Your ad may be promoting a specific page on your site, such as click training. So the display URL might be the website.com for branding purposes, but the actual destination might be this: website.com/dog-training/clicker-training.html.

You'll let Google know what keywords and phrases you're targeting, and you can target them three different ways – broad, exact, phrase matches and negative.

A broad keyword would be like this: dog – but you have to be careful because your ad could show up whenever someone types the word dog in but in any format, like this: Snoop Dogg. Now if you have a dog training site, Snoop Dogg isn't what you're shooting for – he's a rapper.

An exact match would be whenever someone types the keyword phrase into Google exactly as you list it, like this: dog training guide – and the ad only shows up if they type in that phrase exclusively, with no other words.

A phrase match lets your ad show for that phrase, even if it includes other words in the search, like this: best dog training guide (even if your keyword is only dog training guide).

A negative keyword phrase is when you don't want your ad to show up if someone types in a particular phrase. For example, if you wanted to exclude freebie seekers, you might include this negative keyword phrase: -free dog training guide.

Once everything's in place, you'll activate your ads. A team will approve them for you, or reject them and let you know why, but you have to pay a $5 activation fee first. You have to choose how you'll pay – they allow post pay or pre-pay using the following methods:

POST-PAY:
- American Express
- JCB
- MasterCard
- Visa
- Bank account payments (US bank accounts only)
- Debit cards with a MasterCard or Visa logo

PREPAY:
- American Express
- JCB
- MasterCard
- Visa
- Debit cards with a MasterCard or Visa logo

Note: If you use post pay, your ads can start running almost instantly. If you choose prepay, then the funds have to get into Google's account first, which can take up to 5-10 business days.

SOME THINGS TO REMEMBER TO HELP YOU AVOID COSTLY MISTAKES:

Don't waste money fighting for the #1 spot in AdWords. Some entrepreneurs will drive up the bids just to make you quit, so focus on performance instead.

Make sure the ad reflects exactly what you're doing on the page, so that your relevancy score improves. Google takes off points if you're not sticking to the relevant content.

BUYING AD SPACE

Ad space can be almost anywhere on the Internet – a static site, a blog, an email autoresponder, a newsletter, a social networking site, a forum, and more! This is one of those things where you'll need to test the market in small doses to see which method performs better for you, and then increase your efforts on the high conversion ones.

You can use a site like Buy Sell Ads to find publishers who are willing to let you buy ad space on their site. You can also cold call (or email) a site owner and ask them if they would be willing to sell some ad space to you on a monthly basis.

You'll want to know where the ad will be placed on the site. The best place is above the fold, which means the visitor sees it right when they land on the page, instead of having to scroll down.

Payment will vary, so shop around. You might have a broad site charging a ton of money for ad space because they get high volume traffic – but it might be so broad that many of your impressions (people who see the ad), aren't interested.

Then again, you might be able to pay less to a site owner whose blog is highly targeted to what you sell, but they don't get as much traffic. This is often much better for you as an advertiser in terms of conversions (not necessarily click throughs).

Some site owners will charge you by the click while most will charge a flat monthly fee (with discounts often being given if you buy several months in advance). Make sure you get all details in writing.

For email autoresponder ad space or online newsletters, you can go to ezine owner directory sites: www.ezinelisting.com or www.newsletteraccess.com.

Contact them and ask if they sell ad space and how it works. Some will have an image ad, while others will allow you to post a text advertisement. You'll want to know what space you get, how lengthy it can be, and how many subscribers they have.

Sometimes you might Google your keyword and realize that the top page is a social networking site like Squidoo. There's no harm in asking the page owner via email if he or she would like to place a banner ad or text link ad on their lens in exchange for monetary compensation.

Or, seek out niche forums in your market and ask the forum owner if they sell ad space. Sometimes they'll have a specific sidebar or banner ad area, but many have an ad section instead, where you pay a flat fee to run an ad.

Using online tools to market your products and services doesn't have to be intimidating. You can always start over and do something different based on the results that you get from previous efforts.

Chapter

12

14 Sure-Fire Check Lists That Guarantee

"The check is really in the mail"

"Success is a science; if you have the conditions, you get the result." – Oscar Wilde

A re you ready to become a Mail Order Millionaire? I've taken you step-by-step through every phase of the process. Now the rest is up to you.

But to review what I have covered in this book and make it even easier for you to make it big in mail order, in this final chapter, I will summarize key points in a series of checklists.

1. **Check list for finding great mail order offerings:**

   ☐ Does the product have exclusivity? Is it unique? Is it not readily available at regular stores?

   ☐ Is the product's perceived value to the consumer far greater than its basic cost to you? Is there enough profit margin built in?

   ☐ Does the product provide a benefit that is highly desirable and easily understood by the consumer?

2. **How to get necessary start-up money. Consider these possible sources:**

   ☐ Your own savings

   ☐ Bank loan

   ☐ Insurance policy cash value

   ☐ Credit cards

   ☐ Home equity loan

   ☐ Venture capital

3. **Make sure you build in sufficient profit:**

   ☐ How many units will you have to sell to cover all of your costs (cost of goods, advertising/promotion preparation and printing, advertising insertion costs, shipping and handling costs)?

   ☐ How much inventory must you carry?

   ☐ What is the potential for repeat orders? For follow-up sales of related products?

4. **Factors to consider in pricing your offering:**

☐ What is the perceived value of your offer?

Magic Price Points	Ideal Cost of Goods
☐ $7.95 + $1 S & H	$2.25
☐ $14.95 + $2 S & H	$3.00
☐ $19.95 + $2 S & H	$4.50
☐ $39.95 + $3 S & H	$10.00
☐ $69.95 + $3 S & H	$25.00
☐ $97.50 + $3 S & H	$35.00
☐ $134.50, S & H Free	$50.00
☐ $195.00, S & H Free	$75.00

☐ Be sure to charge extra for shipping and handling

☐ Start modestly, to make sure you don't waste money foolishly

5. **Reasons for adding mail order to an existing business:**

☐ Expand your market geographically

☐ Contact marginal prospects not practical for sales force

☐ Reach existing customers more often

☐ Offer retail customers shop-at-home convenience

☐ Build store traffic

☐ Announce promotions

☐ Single out specific prospect groups

☐ Appeal directly to your competitors' customers

6. **Check list for evaluating ads and mailers:**

☐ A I D A

  ☐ Attention

  ☐ Interest

  ☐ Desire

  ☐ Action

7. **What to look for in a winning headline:**

☐ Is it a grabber?

☐ Does it offer the user a strong benefit?

☐ Would it be improved by such magic words as:

  ☐ Now

  ☐ New

  ☐ How to

  ☐ Free

  ☐ Guaranteed

☐ Has your agency or creative source provided several alternative headlines for you to consider?

8. **Check list for effective body copy:**

☐ Does it fulfill the promise of the headline? Is it convincing?

☐ Does it stay interesting/exciting to the very end?

☐ Does it talk directly to "You" the reader?

☐ Is it simply written – short words, short sentences?

☐ Does it read well out loud?

9. **Things to consider before printing:**

☐ Have you checked the creative carefully?

☐ If you're contracting for your own printing, have you secured three competing bids?

10. **Select from types of mailing lists you can use:**

☐ Your own list

☐ Rented lists of competitive product users

☐ Rented lists of companion or similar type product users

☐ Rented lists based on consumers with personal profile characteristics identical to people who use your product, but who have no product purchase history

11. **What can you test?**

☐ Complete mailing package

☐ Advertising copy

☐ Price

☐ Offer

☐ Mailing lists

☐ Individual elements in total package

☐ Response devices

12. **Testing guidelines:**

☐ Test just one element at a time

☐ Test major items only

☐ Test enough circulation to give meaningful results

☐ Don't make big decisions based on little differences in results

☐ Don't read into results factors not included in the test

☐ Don't expect results to be the be-all and end-all

☐ Don't over test

13. **How to select an advertising agency:**

☐ Look through publications that have lots of mail order ads in them

☐ Make a list of mail order advertisers who repeat ads often

☐ Call these advertisers for the name of their agency

☐ Call the publications for names of mail order agencies they work with

☐ Call these agencies, ask for names and phone numbers of their clients you may call for references

☐ Ask for each agency's client list and how long they have served each client

☐ Request name of specific person who would be responsible for your account and meet this person to see if the "chemistry" between you is right.

14. **Preparing to talk to your advertising agency:**

☐ List product points, assign priorities to these points

☐ Put the sales pitch in writing, if one exists

☐ Provide product spec sheet

☐ Furnish file of existing product ads as well as competitors' ads

☐ Turn over any testimonial letters from customers

☐ Give them publicity releases/published articles

☐ Supply sample of product if possible – if not, photograph and/or written instructions on how to use

Now you have all of the tools at your disposal to become a success in mail order. The rest is up to you. As Curtis Grant of Nation's Business Magazine pointed out, even if you have the greatest idea in the

world, it won't do you any good unless you act on it:
"People who want milk shouldn't sit on a stool in the
middle of a field in the hope that a cow will back up to
them."

So, go for it! You too, can become a Mail Order
Millionaire. And many happy returns!

In Summation

"Most people give up just when they're about to achieve success. They quit on the one yard line. They give up at the last minute of the game one foot from a winning touchdown." – Ross Perot

HOW TO BECOME A MAIL ORDER MILLIONAIRE is an easy to follow guide to success in mail order.

Not everyone who reads it will automatically become wealthy because not everyone is willing to put in the time and effort necessary to become wealthy in any venture they undertake.

Mail order is no different.

To become a Mail Order Millionaire you must be willing to work long hours, to take risks, to constantly fine tune the skills you will acquire from each product or service you are associated with, to learn from your failures and to never give up.

You must learn to trust your own instincts, to seek out and use ideas from successful people in the business and most important of all, never underestimate or under appreciate your customer. They tell you something every time you direct an ad or send a mailing out. Learn to listen to what your customer is saying, even when it's negative or results in a "no sale".

This book will help to provide you with a road map to success in mail order, but remember you'll never get there unless you begin taking that first step and then the next and then the next.

You'll gain confidence with every step you take so don't hesitate, begin your journey, and have fun along the way.

Fred Broitman started in mail order as an office boy in a mail order agency in 1952 just before he graduated from high school. He attended Northwestern University.

He learned the skills that have made him one of the most respected authorities in mail order selling from two of the greatest mail order men in the business, Nelson J. McMahon and Paul Grant.

He has been responsible for selling hundreds of millions of dollars in products and services. He is the founder and C.E.O. of Chicago's largest independently owned mail order advertising agency, Sunman Direct.

You can learn more from Fred at his blog: http://becomeamailordermillionaire.com

www.ingramcontent.com/pod-product-compliance
Lightning Source LLC
Chambersburg PA
CBHW070404200326
41518CB00011B/2052